D0629752

RULES,
BRITANNIA

RULES, BRITANNIA

Toni Summers Hargis

Thomas Dunne Books
ST. MARTIN'S PRESS
NEW YORK

THOMAS DUNNE BOOKS.
An imprint of St. Martin's Press.

www.stmartins.com.

Library of Congress Cataloging-in-Publication Data

Hargis, Toni Summers
    Rules, Britannia : an insider's guide to life in the United Kingdom / Toni Summers Hargis.
       p. cm.
    ISBN 0-312-33665-9
    EAN 978-0-312-33665-3
    1. Visitors, Foreign—Great Britain—Life skills guides. 2. Life skills—Great Britain—Handbooks, manuals, etc. 3. Etiquette—Great Britain—Handbooks, manuals, etc. 4. Immigrants—Great Britain—Life skills guides. 5. Great Britain—Social life and customs—Handbooks, manuals, etc. I. Title

DA110 .H335 2006
427—dc22

2005054788

First Edition: March 2006

10 9 8 7 6 5 4 3 2 1

In loving memory of my father, Ronald Selby Summers. An Englishman and a gentleman.

Contents

Acknowledgments

SINCE THIS BOOK has been almost a decade in the making, a lot of people have been involved in its creation—some unwittingly. To every American who ever asked for advice before a trip to the UK, thank you for prompting me to think about the differences. In particular, thanks to my friend Carla Young, whose relocation to England, along with her encouragement to keep writing, planted the seed of this book. Too numerous to mention individually are the friends who have been peppered with questions on anything from female impersonators to fizzy drinks. I am also indebted to Cary Bomier for her thoughtful introduction to my agent. My mother, Veronica Summers, got out the red pen, and added invaluable information, as well as the feedback that she "couldn't put it down." That's what mothers are for! I have benefited enormously from the often whacky American vocabulary of my husband, Mark.

He provided a constant flow of material and patiently answered a million and one questions, sometimes at two in the morning.

Thanks to my publisher, Thomas Dunne, who has been generous and enthusiastic about the book from the very beginning. Finally, a huge thank you to my agent and friend, Nancy Crossman, whose faith and encouragement are truly appreciated.

Introduction

WITH SO MANY excellent books, guides, and Web sites about the United Kingdom, what prompted this book? Actually, it was Americans. Since moving to the States from England in 1990, I have been asked repeatedly to give advice to Americans either relocating to the UK or planning to travel extensively there. I knew from my own relocation experience that much of what they would *really* need to know wouldn't be found in the bookstores. Most of this knowledge comes too late—after you've made the embarrassing mistakes. No one tells you how to avoid making a fool of yourself at weddings; what to expect when being entertained at someone's house; what the office culture will be like; and so on. As my list of "advice" increased, so too did the positive feedback from Americans who read it. Eventually it became obvious that my information on how the Brits *really* live their lives was filling a vital gap for Americans. This is the type of information I could have used when I made my own transatlantic move, and it became my mission to provide the real skinny on life in the United Kingdom.

Rules, Britannia is best described by what it's not than by what it is. It is not a boring old etiquette guide, it is also not a U.S./UK dictionary, and since it doesn't contain advice on where to go and what to see, this book is definitely not a travel guide. I do, however, provide a fairly comprehensive glossary at the end of most chapters, and many Web site references to guide you to useful information elsewhere. As far as is humanly possible, I have filled this book with facts rather than my own pontifications on Americans and Brits. Although many writers have already written hilarious observations about the Brits and British culture, you'll develop your own opinions in no time. Similarly, although classism is alive and well in the UK, I have included all kinds of British words you'll hear while over there, regardless of their social implications.

The book is organized for maximum convenience and user-friendliness. It covers a wide variety of subjects, including driving, shopping, dining out, managing with small children, and taking a vacation. Each chapter deals with a single subject where I give nuggets of information that you won't find elsewhere, followed by a handy list of Brit words to demystify some of what you'll hear. Since my aim is to aid communication between Americans and Brits, I don't include British words that are different but easy to understand. Similarly, I do not caution Americans against using words that the Brits could probably figure out.

Although many UK-themed books contain observations (albeit witty ones) about the Brits, most are written by Americans and often miss the finer points about living in the UK. Only a *true* Brit can give you the real skinny on what to do and what to avoid when staying in the UK.

1

Regions and Their Differences

FIRST THINGS FIRST—the Brits actually don't call themselves Brits. I do here for convenience but would never do it in
the UK. People in the UK tend to say they're English, Irish,
Scottish/Scots, or Welsh. ("Scotch" refers to the drink.) Pass-
ports, however, state the nationality of all people living in the
UK and Northern Ireland as "British." Try asking someone if
they're British, and most "Brits" will correct you and say, "Actually, I'm English, Welsh," and so on. It's basically the same as
lumping Americans and Canadians together.

According to the CIA's *World Fact Book,* the United Kingdom is slightly smaller than Oregon; however, you'll find an
alarming number of regional differences even within a fifty-mile
radius. Like many Brits, I can tell if a person is from my home-
town, or from a town ten miles away, by the accent and use of
different words and phrases. In the Northeast of England, "bon-
nie" means pretty, while further south, in Yorkshire, it can mean

"fat"; as you can see, there's a lot of opportunity to really put your foot in your mouth. "Cannie" describes a really nice person in the Northeast, but in Scotland refers to someone who is street-smart, careful with money, or even sly.

As in the United States, there is a north/south divide in England, although not so much in Northern Ireland, Scotland, and Wales. It's the opposite to the States in that Northerners are the ones who are supposed to be less sophisticated and one step removed from cavemen. A closer look at the UK however, reveals a much more complex fabric.

The north/south question is very subjective and partly driven by snobbery. The southern joke is that the north begins at Watford, a mere thirty miles north of London. As someone from the far north east of England, I am bunched together with people from Manchester and Birmingham as "northerners" and yet I have nothing in common with them other than not being from London. In fact, Birmingham is far closer to London than it is to Newcastle. To me, Birmingham is not in the north of England, being geographically situated less than halfway up.

If you travel around the UK for any length of time, you will soon appreciate the differences from one region to another, both in culture and accent.

Sometimes the accents are so different that people from opposite ends of the country (a mere one thousand or so miles) can barely understand each other. People from Glasgow and Cornwall might as well be speaking in different languages. There's not a lot I can do to help you here, except warn you that you will be faced with seemingly unintelligible conversation from time to time. Unfortunately, asking the speaker to slow down rarely makes him or her more intelligible.

Bear in mind also that most Brits are only used to hearing the generic American accent of TV shows. You may think you don't have an accent, but the look on people's faces when you talk to them will soon set you straight. If you *know* you have a heavy accent, save yourself hours of repetition and slow down! Having said that, be prepared to repeat yourself when addressing someone for the first time. They're usually concentrating more on the fact that you have a strange accent than on the words you're using. On some occasions you'll even see the mouth drop open a few inches.

Unlike Americans, the Brits don't really pay a lot of attention to their ancestry, since most of them have lived in the same country for many generations. If you say you're Italian or Irish, but are speaking with an undeniable American accent, there'll be a look or two of skepticism from any Brits around. If you have a strong southern accent, but say you're *from* New York, expect some confusion or disbelief. That's because if you ask a Brit where she's from, you'll likely be told her birthplace rather than where she lives now.

Often, the regions, cities, and their inhabitants have nicknames, which are used regularly in the UK:

- Birmingham—the people are called *"Brummies"* and the accent is *"Brummy."* Birmingham is sometimes referred to as *"Brum."* The area around Birmingham is also known as the Black Country.
- The Black Country—comprises the areas north and west of Birmingham, but not Birmingham itself.
- Blighty—nickname for England, from the Hindu *bilayati* meaning "foreign."
- Border country—refers to the counties of England and

Scotland on either side of the border, or the border between Wales and England.

- The Broads, or Norfolk Broads—a stretch of very flat land in the county of Norfolk, near the seaside town of Great Yarmouth, on the east coast.
- Bristol—the residents are Bristolians and their accent is Bristolian. However, because of the accent, Bristol sometimes sounds like "Brizzle." (People from the West Country in general are often referred to as "carrot crunchers.")
- Channel Isles—off the French coast of Normandy, in the English Channel; they comprise Guernsey, Jersey, Alderney, Sark, Herm, and a handful of smaller islands.
- Fen country—refers to Lincolnshire and parts of Cambridgeshire; here the land is extremely flat and boggy.
- Glasgow (by the way, it's pronounced "Glazzgo," not "Glass Cow")—the people are Glaswegians ("Glazweejans"), and their accent is unintelligible. (Just kidding!)
- Home Counties—refers to the counties surrounding London, whence many people commute into the City.
- The Isle of Man—both the people and the accent are called Manx; there is also a Manx cat that has no tail.
- The Lakes—the Lake District, on the northwest border of England and Scotland.
- Liverpool—people living there are either Liverpudlians or Scousers. Their accent is called "Scouse" (soft "s"). The region is Merseyside (pronounce the first "s" like a "z").
- London (which is a city, not a town)—the residents are generally known as Londoners, although you can call yourself a Cockney if you were born within the sound of Bow Bells. St. Mary-le-Bow Church (or Bow Church) is situated

in Cheapside. London is sometimes referred to as "The Smoke."

- Manchester—there you'll find Mancunians (hard "c"); their accent is Mancunian.
- The Midlands—southerners think the Midlands start just north of London, but this is really the area around Birmingham, Coventry, and Leicester.
- Newcastle-upon-Tyne—The people are called Geordies ("Jordies") and they have a Geordie accent. The region is Tyneside.
- The Northeast—The northeast of England: the cities of Newcastle, Durham, Sunderland, York, and surrounding areas.
- The Peak District—an area in the middle of England, between Sheffield and Manchester; a favorite of walkers and nature lovers.
- The Pennines—the area of England around the Pennine Mountains, in the mid-Northeast.
- The Potteries—a group of small towns in Staffordshire making up Stoke-on-Trent.
- The provinces—anywhere outside London.
- The Shetlands and the Orkneys—small groups of remote islands off the northern tip of Scotland.
- Snowdonia—the mountain region in the west of Wales.
- The Western Isles—remote islands off the west coast of Scotland.

Remember that, just as your knowledge of British geography might not be very detailed, the Brits won't know where many places are in the USA, other than the big cities. In particular, regional names or nicknames will be totally foreign to them. These include Cajun, Canuck, Cheesehead, Creole, Hoozier, Polack, redneck, wet back, and any references to Native Americans or the Mason-Dixon line. Also, since there are not as many Spanish speakers living in the UK, assume that most Brits won't know even a few words in Spanish—French, German, or Latin, perhaps, but not Spanish!

NAME PRONUNCIATION

Many place names in the United Kingdom have extremely peculiar spellings, and even the Brits don't know how to pronounce them all. However, there are a few key places that you might want to pronounce correctly, or at least recognize the correct pronunciation when you hear it. If you are traveling in Wales, Scotland, and parts of the Southwest, the place names may be in Welsh, Gaelic, or Cornish, and any attempt at pronunciation will be painful to you and the locals. It's best to do what every other visitor does—ask or point!

Most Welsh places beginning with "double ell" are impossible to attempt unassisted. Best bet is to have a few lessons from a friendly, Welsh-speaking native—in the pub if possible. It's a fantastic language to listen to and your attempts will provide hours of mirth to you and your coach. I lived in Wales as a small child, and I'm just glad the place was called Criccieth.

You might thank me for these pointers:

- "Folk"—Any place name with "-folk" on the end is pronounced as in the four-letter expletive rather than "foke." I kid you not! Therefore places like Norfolk and Suffolk are in fact pronounced "Norfuk" and "Suffuk."

- "Ford"—Names of places with "ford" in them are truncated. You don't pronounce this word as you would the car maker, but squash it together and simply pronounce the "f" and the "d." Examples of such places include Hertford (pronounced "Hartfd"), Dartford, and Hereford. However, if you come across a place *beginning* with "Ford," you pronounce the word as in the car maker—e.g., Fordham, except the "h" would be silent (see below). Got it?

- "Ham"—Brits more or less ignore the "-ham" found at the end of many place names. Birmingham is pronounced "Birming'm." Nottingham becomes "Notting'm." Other examples include Fulham in London (Full'm), Durham (Dur'm), and Dagenham (Dagen'm).

- "Mouth"—Anything ending with "-mouth" is pronounced "muth." E.g., Plymouth is "Plimuth" (not rhyming with "fly"), Weymouth is "Waymuth," and Portsmouth is "Portsmuth." Since the "mouth" part of the name refers to the mouth of a river, you'll usually find these places on the coast somewhere. An exception I can think of (and there are surely more) is Tynemouth, which is pronounced as you'd expect.

- "Shire"—Any county (and they are all counties) that ends with "-shire" is not pronounced that way. For example, most people pronounce "Leicestershire" as "Lestershu" or "Lestersha"; Yorkshire is pronounced "Yorkshu" or "Yorksha." (Basically, what I'm trying to do here is to cut short the sound of the "shire" part.) Confusingly, sometimes the "shire" is pronounced more like "sheer."

- "Wich"—Unfortunately, place names ending in "-wich" can either have the "w" pronounced—or not. I can help you out with a few of them, but others will no doubt trip you up. Greenwich, in London, is pronounced "Grenidge," while the Aldwych is the "Aldwidge." Sandwich, in Kent, is pronounced like the one you eat.
- "Wick"—Most names ending in "-wick" have a silent "w." Berwick and Alnwick, both near the English/Scottish border, are pronounced "Berrick" and "Annick." Warwick is "Warrick," and Chiswick in London is "Chizzick."
- Berkshire is pronounced "Barkshu" or "Barksha." Its real name is Royal Berkshire, but people usually drop the royal bit. You'll also hear it simply referred to as Berks (pronounced "Barks") from time to time.
- Derby and Derbyshire—Pronounced "Darby" and "Darbyshu" or "Darbysha."
- Edinburgh—The "G" in this word is silent. People say "Edinbura" or "Edinbru"; either would be understood. What you tend not to hear is "Edinburrow."
- Glasgow—Pronounced "Glazz Go" as opposed to "Glass Cow." I hate to be picky about this, but it drives the natives crazy.
- Gloucester and Gloucestershire—pronounced "Gloster" and "Glostershu/Glostersha." Definitely *not* "Glowsestershire."
- Hampshire—This, you'll be pleased to learn, is pronounced as you'd expect; don't forget to truncate the "shire," though. Some people will say they live in Hants instead of Hampshire. Don't ask me where the "n" comes from. Similarly, Northamptonshire is often called North Hants.

- Hertford and Hertfordshire—Both are pronounced as in "heart." Don't forget not to say "ford" but "fd." If you can pronounce Herefordshire correctly, you've been paying attention. It would be pronounced "Hartfdsha"! Again, you might hear someone saying they live in Herts (pronounced "Hearts"), and this would also be Hertfordshire.
- Leicester—Both the city and the square in London are pronounced "Lester." Similarly, Bicester is pronounced "Bisster."
- Loughborough is pronounced "Luffbura."
- Shrewsbury is pronounced "Shroosbury" or "Shrowsbree," depending on where you come from.
- Slough is pronounced "Slow," rhyming with "cow."
- The river that runs through London is the Thames. The "h" is ignored and the "a" sounds like "e." Pronounce it "Tems." (Really!)

You'll also need to know that Scots are often called "Joch" or "Jock," the Welsh "Taffy," and the Irish "Paddy." There seems to be no common name given to the English, although the term "Joe Bloggs" or "Joe Soap" is the English equivalent of John Doe.

And finally, I'm not saying this to alarm you, but the Brits use different names for the same things depending on where they live. As an American, you may know what a scallion is. In the UK it is called a spring onion and many southerners have never even heard the alternative word "scallion." If you are going to be staying in a specific region for any length of time, do yourself a favor and buy a local destination guide when you get there. Also look up the place on the Internet, as there are usually

Web sites for and by locals, which will give you a flavor of the region, as well as a more local vocabulary.

RESOURCES

www.knowhere.co.uk—The Knowhere Guide's Web site, a user's guide to Britain, often written by the inhabitants. Calls itself "not your typical tourist guide."

2

Words That Guarantee Giggles

THERE ARE MANY WORDS in the United States that you say every day without a second thought that will sound hilarious to the Brits. There are also words in their vocabulary that will crease you up. My favorite, for some reason, is the American "behoove." Not sure why, but it just cracks me up every time I hear it! And you have to admit that the British "behove" has a slightly more intelligent ring to it. (Oops, there I go, pontificating again!)

My purpose in forewarning you about these words is not to deprive you of a good laugh, but to help prevent inappropriate laughter, since many of these words come up in serious, professional settings. (Well, okay, not the first one!)

- Lasso/lassoo—Americans say "lasso" and Brits "lassoo." I suppose, since there are far fewer cowboys in the UK, the American version is correct, but don't tell the Brits that—and don't laugh too loudly!

- Also expect a few titters when you say the word "herb." The Brits pronounce the "h" and to them, "erb" sounds like half a word. Incidentally, when speaking British English, you can always hear the "h" in "human" but not in "vehicle." Also quite funny is the fact that the Brits say "titbit" while Americans say "tidbit"; and the American "hodge-podge" becomes "hotchpotch." Then of course there's "schedule"—Americans all over the planet get the biggest kick out of the British version, pronounced "shedyool."

- Van Gogh—people from both sides of the pond will laugh at the way the other side pronounces this name. The Brits say "Van Goff " and the "Goff " part is pronounced as in "off " rather than "go." When they hear an American saying "Van Go," some Brits might not even understand whom you're talking about. And you'll be surprised how many times this name comes up in coversation.

  While we're discussing artists, the Brits pronounce Monet slightly differently. The "o" sounds more like the "o" in coffee, and the emphasis is on the first syllable. Of course, when an American says "coffee," it doesn't sound anything like the way the Brits say "Monet," and you could end up discussing Manet.

- Several other seemingly similar words will cause mutual chuckles when they're pronounced out loud. For "yogurt" the Brits pronounce the first syllable like "fog" rather than "go"; "pasta" and "basil" are pronounced with a flat "a," as in "fast"; "oregano" has the emphasis on the third syllable rather than the second. Perhaps one of the funniest to the Brits will be the American pronunciation of "buoy," and I guarantee they won't know what the heck you're talking about unless you're actually pointing at one. They pronounce it "boy," and since it's not a word that comes up on American TV shows too often, you'll be able to count on one hand the number of Brits who have ever heard your version of its pronunciation—if you say "boowee," that is! "Pianist," in the UK, only has two distinct syllables, making it sound more like "penis" to the American ear.

- The first time I heard about "Fat Tuesday," I fell about. The Brits call it Pancake Tuesday, or Shrove Tuesday.

- The office is also good for a few nervous giggles: in the UK people ask for a "rise" in salary, and use a "rubber" to erase their errors.

- The Brits refer to their underpants as "pants" and their outer garments as "trousers." Asking someone's opinion, for example, on what pants you should wear for the office party will probably cause confusion or embarrassment, and most definitely, nervous giggles.

- Little girls wear "panties," grown women do not. I still cannot bring myself to call my underwear "panties," and you'll probably receive some odd looks with this one. "Knickers" is the most common word, although others you may come across include "underwear," "briefs," and "smalls."

- The Brits often refer to their pet German Shepherds as "Alsatians," which, for some reason, Americans find hilarious. Beats me, but there you go. Also on the subject of animals, while we all call unnaturally white animals "albinos," the Brits often pronounce this word "albeeno."

- If you're about to bang your head against a four-foot beam in an Old Tudor pub, you'll very likely be told to "Mind your head." Similarly, at some stations on the London Underground system, you'll hear the announcement, "Mind the gap." This is basically warning you of the foot-wide gap between the train and the platform. On the other hand, if you use the word "mind" to mean paying heed to someone (as in "These children should mind their mother"), it probably won't be understood.

- My American husband always gets a kick out of the way the Brits respond to the question, "How are you?" Unlike in America, where everyone says "Great" or variations thereof, the Brits will usually tell you *exactly* how they are—ailments and all. If they're feeling pretty good, they will allow themselves a modest "Oh, not too bad, thank you." Don't be offended by the lack of enthusiasm in their responses, and also don't be surprised when your extremely enthusiastic "Happy to be here" (my husband's mantra) is suspected of being a sarcastic response. Incidentally, when saying, "How are you?" to someone in the UK, you are ex-pected to wait for a response. It is not used simply as a passing greeting in the way Americans do at home.

- I guarantee that if you address a British woman as "Ma'am" she will think you're trying to be funny, although calling a male "sir" is not so hilarious for some reason. Similarly, the southern practice of children addressing women as Miss Toni, Miss Susan, and so on, is not done in the UK.

- If your name is Randy, be prepared to be teased ad nau-seam in the UK. Randy is not a name and basically means "horny." During his active bachelor years, Prince Andrew, the queen's second son, was nicknamed "Randy Andy" by the British press. Although males are sometimes called Willy, this word means "penis," so again, be prepared for titters.

- Other names that do not exist as names in the UK, and that will cause mirth, are: Trey, Clay, Stone, Wood—words usually reserved for inanimate objects. Family names (such as Madison, Macadden, etc.) are generally not used as first names, especially for girls. Girls are also rarely called Michael, Courtney, and Sean/Shawn, although Kelly is always female. Tracey, Lyn or Lin, Carroll, and Rosie would never, ever be used for males. Incidentally, first names are usually referred to as Christian names and second names are surnames.

• On the other hand, you'll hear some very odd names while over there, and I'm not just talking about the Gaelic ones. Vivien and Hilary can be used as boys' names, although that's not so common any more. The girl's name Jill is often spelled with a "G" (short for Gillian). The "Gill" spelling would never indicate a male, as the name Gil is not common in the UK. Many moons ago, while planning to attend a training course in the United States, an English friend called Gill tried numerous times to explain to the administrators that she was in fact female. Sure enough, when we all got to the training center, she found her room miles away from the rest of us—tucked away on the men's floor. None of us could figure out why at the time. Another English friend, also called Gill, has recently legally changed her name to Jill. She travels a lot to the States, and her ticket nearly always showed her as Jill, which never matched her passport. In these days of heightened security, she often had to pony up the $100 or so to have her ticket and passport match.

• There are also some very odd phrases in the UK, which might make you think of something completely different from what is intended. One that instantly springs to mind is "Keep your pecker up," which simply means keep your spirits up! "Codswallop" is one you will hear from time to time, which is a politer form of "bullshit." If you're told you have "egg on your chin," you should immediately check your flies—it means your zipper's undone!

- Some of the place names you'll hear are so weird you'll think you're being taken for a fool. Examples include, but are certainly not limited to: "Bottoms," in West Yorkshire; "Zeal Monarchorum" in Devon; "Yetts O' Muckhart" and "Pool of Muckhart" in Scotland; "Salt" in Staffordshire; "Upper Slaughter" and "Lower Slaughter" in Gloucestershire; "Crawley Down" in West Sussex; "Old Leake" in Lincolnshire; "Child's Ercall" in Shropshire; and my favorite, "Chipping Sodbury" in Gloucestershire (often referred to as Sodding Chipbury). Finally, the most northerly point in the UK is "Muckle Flugga" in the Shetland Isles. Can you believe that one? Keep a Road Atlas handy at all times in case you need to entertain yourself for a few hours!

- People in the UK love to name their houses. I once knew a family who lived in a house called "The Butts," which caused no ripples in the UK. You'll also find the odd joker who calls his house something like "Costa Plenty" or "Dunroamin'."

3

Words That Guarantee Embarrassment

ON ONE OF my mother's first visits to my home in the States, she asked my husband if he'd mind "knocking her up at eight in the morning." I don't care to reflect on what was going through his mind, and the embarrassment on my mother's face when the error was explained was priceless! In most cases using the wrong word may cause laughter or confusion, but it won't be fatal. However, there are some American words and practices that will guarantee you're not invited back for dinner. Many things that are acceptable in the States may appear rude and ill-mannered in the UK. Here are a few:

- Although it can mean to get someone pregnant, the phrase "to knock someone up" can also be a fairly mild request in the UK for one person to knock on another person's bedroom door in the morning. Brits can also be known to "knock up a quick meal." As you can imagine, most

Americans react with varying degrees of disbelief and embarrassment the first time they hear these variations.

- I say quite confidently that probably the biggest shocker to the Brits is when Americans refer to a person as "she" or "he" when that person is standing right in front of them or is within earshot. I simply can't emphasize how rude this is. Use the person's name, and if you can't remember it, the trick is to say, "We were just discussing..." In fact, Brits will jump through linguistic hoops to avoid using the personal pronoun in this situation. Even when they know that Americans mean no offense, Brits still can't believe it is actually being said. Again, I must stress that this is *so* rude! A common response to the use of "she" will be the question, "Who's she, the cat's mother?" (Despite heroic efforts on my part, I have yet to come across the root of this phrase, although it apparently made its debut in the *Oxford English Dictionary* at the end of the nineteenth century.)

- Americans are far more open about discussing salary levels and money in general. Brits are generally uncomfortable talking about how much money they have or make and it could appear "brash" to do so. Asking someone how much they earn or what they paid for their house would put most Brits in a dreadful "spot," but you might get your answer as they're not very good at fluffing, and would worry that declining to answer would offend. They are similarly reticent about discussing house prices if they are buying or selling.

- "Fanny" relates to the female private parts and is an *extremely* crude word—not even used as a slang term. Even though most Brits will know that you are referring to the derrière, it will still draw shocked looks. This word should not be used in front of children. Also to be avoided is the term "fanny pack"—the Brits call it a "bum bag."

I recently read about Ada Doggett, a lady from Arlington, Texas, who was famed for designing the perfect Miss America swimsuit. Apparently Ada is also credited with the idea of *spraying the contestants' fannies with glue* so the bathing suit would stay in place. Can you imagine the tears that brought to this Brit's eyes?

- Another word that should really not be said in front of children and/or in decent company is "bugger." In the UK, this is never used to describe anything that comes out of one's nose, and is purely and simply an extremely offensive word. Sometimes you'll hear someone say "Bugger off" (meaning "Scram"), which for some reason is slightly more acceptable than the "b" word on its own. Even more often you'll hear someone say they have "bugger all," which means "nothing." My advice is to avoid this word until you're confident of its place in society.

- "Butt," though not a curse word, is still viewed as crude and would certainly not be expected to pop out of the mouths of your offspring. Seriously, though, if your kids tend to use a lot of American slang (butt, fart, crud, crap, asshole, and beyond), you might find that they aren't asked to many playdates for fear they will teach the other kids these crude expressions.

- Unless you really mean to cause offense or cuss, never use the word "freakin." In the UK, the alternative "F" word is "frigging," and, well, "freakin" sounds much too close. "Frigging" is almost as inappropriate as the real thing. I still cannot believe the amount of times I hear decent, upstanding Americans say "freakin" and constantly have to reassure myself that it's acceptable in the United States.

- Another innocent word that could cause real offense is "towhead." This is not known in the UK; the most similar sounding word (especially when referring to children) is "toe-rag," which means "brat" and is extremely insulting. To add to the confusion, Brits will wonder why you are smiling beatifically at their kids while calling them such a rude name. Incidentally, referring to military children as "army brats" will sound terribly offensive to Brits.

- Despite the popularity of the Austin Powers movies, the terms "shag," "shagging," or even "shagadelic" are not considered "nice" in the UK. And if you ever mention the practice of "shagging flies" to a Brit, goodness only knows what they will think Americans do in their spare time.

- A "rubber" in England is an eraser; so don't be alarmed or embarrassed when your friend's cute five-year-old daughter asks you if you have one. You may also experience a request for a rubber many times in an office situation, and at your kids' school.

- Political correctness is not as de rigueur in the UK as in the United States. You may hear jokes (even on TV) that you would never hear in public in the States. Although Americans generally think the Brits are very reserved and polite, you will quickly discover that they are far more direct in many cases. Even commercials in the UK are more risqué than you tend to see in the States. When watching British TV shows, particularly serious dramas, be prepared for a full frontal or two at any moment. Obviously this will not occur during children's viewing time, but after 9 p.m.

there's no telling. If you're not convinced, try tuning in to Graham Norton's talk show (chat show) on BBC America and see how crude your usually PC American celebrities are when they think no Americans are watching.

- Although the stereotype of the loud American (wearing plaid trousers) is somewhat exaggerated, the decibel level of conversations in the UK is considerably lower than in the United States. Brits usually avoid "sharing" with strangers around them. When in the company of Brits, avoid embarrassing them (and yourself) and talk as quietly as everyone else—especially in restaurants.

  Years ago, my husband and I were at a corporate event in Paris. We sat in the hotel foyer people-watching for a while (okay, nursing a drink), and began trying to guess the nationality of people as they came through the door. Not very difficult in some cases, I'm afraid. In general, the Asian guests spoke so quietly they looked like they were lip-synching; the Europeans were only audible when they were a few feet from us; but the Americans could be heard before they were seen. I kid you not!

- In the UK, to "nurse" a baby simply means to hold and cuddle it. So, if someone hands you their precious bundle and asks, "Would you mind nursing the baby while I get tea?", just smile graciously and do your best.

- Still on the baby theme, the name of the nipple of a baby's bottle in the UK is "teat." If you say "nipple," people will look mildly shocked and then won't be quite sure how to respond.

- Be prepared to qualify your meaning if talking about a trip to an American strip mall. This phrase is not known in the UK and your listeners will assume you frequent strip joints on a casual basis!

- If introduced to someone called Stephen, Susan, David, or Elizabeth (for example), don't then address him or her as Steve, Sue, Dave, or Liz. Fewer nicknames are used in the UK and people generally introduce themselves by the name they would like you to use. Shortening names will be considered overfamiliar or just plain weird. Incidentally, if Charles is shortened, it's usually to Chaz or Charlie, rather than Chuck.

- While the "middle finger" gesture is understood in the UK, the common equivalent is the two-fingered V-sign. The index and middle fingers are formed into a "V," the palm faces inward, and the hand is invariably thrust upward. It is just as offensive as its American counterpart. Americans attempting the "V for Victory" sign (where the palm faces outward) should be sure to distinguish between the two V-signs, as more than a few American politicians have unwittingly told the British public exactly where to go!

4

Words That Guarantee Confusion

DURING YOUR TIME in the UK, there will be many, many words and phrases you'll hear that will leave you totally baffled. Although we're all supposed to be speaking English, American friends of mine who've lived in the UK for years tell me they're still confused on a daily basis. Such words and phrases include (but will not be limited to):

- **Aggro** *n*—trouble ("I didn't want any aggro"), from the word "aggravation"
- **All to pot (or gone to pot)**—something has gone very wrong
- **Argy-bargy** *n*—trouble; like "aggro"
- ***Arse** *n*—ass; butt
- ***Arse over tit (falling)**—head over heels, literally

*Not "nice" language.

- **"As the actress said to the bishop"**—phrase used when a double entendre has been said; a bit like the Monty Python "Nudge nudge, wink, wink"
- **Backshee/buckshee** *a*—free, costing nothing (from the Indian *backsheesh*)
- **Barmy** *a*—mad, stupid
- **Belt up**—shut up
- **Berk** *n*—idiot
- **Bloke** *n*—man, guy
- **Bloody** *a*—used to express anger, shock or as emphasis; an alternative to "extremely"
- **Bloody Nora**—an expression of surprise or shock
- **Blot your copybook**—to damage your own reputation
- **Blower** *n*—telephone; "on the blower" (mainly in the south)
- **Bob** *n*—shilling in pre-decimal currency; older people might still say something cost "five bob" = 25 new pence
- **"Bob's your Uncle"**—"There you have it"—a phrase used to end a sentence definitively
- **Bog standard** *a*—typical, run-of-the-mill
- **Bonce** *n*—head
- **Brassed off** *a*—fed up
- **Brass Monkey weather**—very, very cold (Challenge: find out the derivation of this phrase)
- **Browned off** *a*—fed up
- ***Bugger all**—nothing—"I've got bugger all to show for my efforts." Not a phrase that should be used in a professional meeting but okay at the pub
- **Cack-handed**—clumsy; not very dexterous
- **Cadge** *v*—to bum, borrow something

- **Cake-hole** *n*—mouth (pie hole)
- **Carrying the can** *v*—to take responsibility/blame for something
- **Chalk and cheese**—two things (or people) that are extremely unalike
- **Chat up** *v*—to hit on
- **Cheers**—salutation when drinking; can also mean thank you
- **Cheerio**—good-bye
- **Cheesed off** *a*—fed up
- **Chucking it down**—raining heavily
- **Chuffed** *a*—very pleased
- **Claptrap** *n*—rubbish
- **Cobblers!**—Rubbish!
- **Cock-a-hoop** *a*—very pleased
- **Cock a snoot (at something or someone)** *v*—to show disrespect for someone by doing something insulting
- ***Cock-up** *n*—a mess ("What a cock-up!")
- ***Cock up** *v*—to mess up ("You've gone and cocked it up now, mate!")
- **Collywobbles (to have the)**—to be very nervous
- **Crackers** *a*—mad, insane
- **Daft** *a*—silly, stupid
- **Deffo**—short for "definitely"
- **Do a bunk**—to run away or escape from somewhere
- **Doddle** *n*—very easy ("It's a doddle, mate")
- **Dodgy** *a*—questionable ("That was a dodgy decision"); not very stable ("That table looks a bit dodgy"); can also refer to someone or something that's not quite legitimate, e.g., "A dodgy character"

- **Donkey's years**—a very long time; often shortened to "donkey's"
- **Effing and blinding** *v*—swearing profusely
- **Faff** *v*—to fuss about
- **Faff** *n*—someone who fusses a lot
- **Fortnight** *n*—two weeks (literally, fourteen nights)
- **Geezer** *n*—man
- **Gippy tummy** *n*—upset stomach
- **Give someone gyp (jip)**—to scold someone
- **Glad-rags** *n*—party clothes
- **Gob** *n*—mouth ("Gobsmacked" means stunned, as in "hit in the mouth")
- **Gob** *v*—to spit; you would "gob" on something—if you were extremely coarse!
- **Gooseberry (playing)** *n*—third wheel on a date
- **Gormless** *a*—dumb; one short of a six-pack
- **Gutted** *a*—very upset, disappointed
- **"I should cocoa"**—rhyming slang for "I should say so"
- **Joe Bloggs/Joe Soap**—John Doe
- **Knickers in a twist** *a*—agitated
- **Knackered** *a*—extremely tired or broken; generally "knackered" *things* are broken, but "knackered" *people* are tired
- **Knacker's yard** *n*—glue factory
- **Knees up** *n*—a fun party
- **Knocked for six**—cricket term meaning either knocked out or very shocked
- **Naff** *a*—crass, hokey
- **"Not my cup of tea"**—not for me; not my style
- **Not on**—not right; usually refers to someone's behavior
- **On my tod**—on my own

- **Over the moon** *a*—very happy
- **Pack in** *v*—to quit doing something—"I've packed in smoking"
- **"Pack it in"**—"Stop that!"
- **Palava** *n*—fuss; pronounced with a long "a" in the middle— you'll hear, "What a palava!"
- *****Piss off** *v*—"Go away!"
- *****Pissed** *a*—drunk; (it never means angry)
- *****Pissed off** *a*—angry
- **Plastered** *a*—drunk
- **Plonker** *n*—idiot
- **Po-faced** *a*—humorless; stern-looking
- **Prat** *n*—dork, etc.
- **Pull your socks up**—Try harder
- **Quid** *n*—one pound (sterling)
- **Ropey** *a*—dicey
- **Ruddy**—a politer version of "bloody"
- **Scarper** *v*—to run away
- *****Scrubber** *n*—prostitute
- **Sent to Coventry**—to send someone to Coventry means to ignore him or her
- *****Shag** *n & v*—sexual intercourse (generally inappropriate for regular conversation)
- **Skint** *a*—out of money, broke
- *****Slag** *n*—derogatory term for a woman, implying she is "loose"
- **Slap-head** *n*—bald person (chrome dome)
- *****Slapper** *n*—another term for a loose woman
- **Snap!**—a children's card game, but the term is also used when two things are the same

- **Snog** *v*—to make out
- *****Sod** *n*—a term of abuse, similar to "bastard"
- *****"Sod it"**—"The hell with it!"
- *****"Sod off "**—"Beat it!"
- *****Sodding** *a*—similar to "bloody"
- **Sticky wicket**—another cricket term meaning a difficult situation
- **Stroppy** *a*—belligerent
- **Swot** *n*—somewhat nerdy person who studies a lot
- **Swot** *v*—to study very hard prior to exams
- **Spon/spondoolix** *n*—money
- **Ta**—thank you
- **Tara**—good-bye
- **Tart** *n*—loose woman
- **Tart up** *v*—to make something look better
- **Ta-ta**—good-bye
- **Take the mickey** *v*—to tease someone
- *****Take the piss** *v*—to tease someone
- **Tenterhooks (to be on)** *n*—pins and needles
- *****Tosspot** *n*—jerk
- *****Tosser** *n*—jerk
- **Waffle (on)** *v*—to talk without thought or meaning
- **Waffle** *n*—irrelevant or meaningless talk (or written work, like homework!)
- *****Wank** *v*—to masturbate
- *****Wanker** *n*—jerk
- **Wee** *n*—urine
- **Wee** *a*—Scots word for "small"
- **Wee** *v*—to urinate

AMERICANISMS TO AVOID

I am not suggesting that you cut all Americanisms from your dialogue while in the UK; indeed, the Brits would be most disappointed if you did that. However, there are a few American phrases you should avoid, as they are totally meaningless to the Brits. Not only will they draw blank looks but any guess hazarded would be completely incorrect. For example, most Brits would interpret the phrase "striking out" as something good, because the phrase "striking lucky" would come to mind. Phrases that are rooted in American history, politics, or sports will usually receive blank looks. After more than a decade in the States, I still have to be reminded of the meaning of words like "carpetbagger" and "bought the farm," since to my mind the actual words hold no clue as to their meaning.

Avoid using the following words and phrases unless with Brits who are extremely "bilingual." Alternatively, if you're in need of a good laugh, try asking a Brit what any of the following words/phrases means:

- Any references to the Cleavers, *Gilligan's Island,* Andy Griffith, Ozzie and Harriet, Mr. Rogers. In fact, if you're going to refer to anything from popular culture, I would advise you to ask if your audience has even heard of it/them before launching into a tale or a joke. You'll be amazed at what didn't make it across the pond (as well as what did).
- Ball park figure
- Behind the eight ball
- Bone up on

- Boonies/boondocks
- Boondoggle
- Bought the farm
- Brown bagging
- Candy striper
- Carpetbagger
- Catty-corner
- Charlie horse
- Cherry picker
- Copacetic
- Cowpoke
- Crying Uncle
- Dixie cup
- Dog and pony show
- Doo hickey
- Druthers (as in "If I had my druthers . . .")
- Dude ranch
- Dukes (as in "Put 'em up")
- Flip the bird
- Hail Mary—when not referring to the Catholic prayer
- Hitting pay dirt
- Home run
- Hoosier
- John Hancock
- Indian giver
- Left field
- Limey
- Mom and apple pie
- Monday morning quarterback
- On the lam
- 'Ornery

- Patsy
- Plain vanilla (bland)
- Pocketbook
- Pork or pork barrel
- Punt—only refers to a form of boating
- Rain check
- Shoo-in
- Shoot the breeze
- Skinny (the)
- SOB
- SOL
- Step up to the plate
- Straw man
- Striking out
- Touch base (somewhat known)
- Uncle Sam
- "101" (as in the basics)

I would refrain from referring to sports teams, players, and so on unless conducting a lecture-type discussion. Just remind yourself that you probably wouldn't recognize names from the world of British rugby, soccer (called football), or most other sports, nor would you know the rules.

SAME WORD, DIFFERENT MEANING

As if it's not confusing enough, Americans and Brits often use the same word and *think* they're talking about the same thing. I find this to be far more dangerous than the simpler misunderstandings discussed previously. You can waste hours debating something, only to find that you're actually having a violent agreement—all because of an assumption that you were speaking the same language!

The "biggies" are:

- **Anxious**—In the UK this means worried or uneasy. Although the *Shorter Oxford English Dictionary* includes "eager" as one of its meanings, Brits would never say they were "anxious" to meet someone when they were actually looking forward to it.
- **Co-ed**—Since this word is actually short for "co-educational," in the UK it is only ever used in that sense. Brits would never describe bathrooms, for example, as co-ed, nor would they refer to a human as a co-ed.
- **Cute**—In the UK, babies might be cute, but strapping twenty-year-old males definitely would not. If you describe any adult as "cute," people will think you mean he or she is sweet perhaps, but not great-looking.
- **Dear**—This word is often used in the UK to mean "pricey." Yes, they also use it to mean cherished, but when talking about something they have just purchased, they're probably complaining about the price!
- **Dirt/Soil**—Americans often refer to the stuff in their flowerbeds as "dirt." The Brits would be horrified at this image since dirt is something you'd sweep up and dispose of. Soil is the only thing (apart from compost, etc.) that you'd find in their gardens.
- **Fag**—Although the American meaning is catching on over there, this word still usually refers to a cigarette! Another British meaning is the practice in older private (public)

schools of having the younger boys perform domestic chores for the older boys. The young boys are called fags. This is the stuff of many a Dickens-type novel and on the way out now, but also probably where the U.S. meaning originated.

- **Fanny**—In the UK, the word "fanny" refers to female genitalia. Even though most Brits know that the American version means one's bottom, I would still strongly advise not using this word—ever! It is a very crude word indeed.

- **Favors**—When I had my first baby, Americans used to ask me whom she "favored." The first time I tried to respond, it went something like, "Well, she spends more time with me than with her daddy right now, so I suppose she might want me around a little more, but that doesn't mean she prefers me." What? While the dictionaries list "resemble" as one meaning, you have probably gleaned by now that this meaning is not generally used. "To favor" (spelled "favour") means to prefer one person to another, and is therefore an incredibly difficult question for a new parent.

- **First floor**—In the UK, the ground floor is, as the name suggests, on ground level. The first floor is above that floor, and is what Americans would call the second floor. When trying to find a floor in a store or hotel, think one floor up. So, if you're directed to the second floor, you should actually be looking for the third floor off the ground.

- **Homely**—Calling someone "homely" in the UK is not particularly offensive. It's not a common word, but when used, it means unpretentious and sometimes plain, never ugly.

- **Ill/Sick**—You literally swap these two around to get your meaning: To "be sick" in the UK means to throw up, so expect looks of disbelief and/or horror when you say you were sick for two weeks. If someone is ill in the UK, it is likely to be a fairly serious condition.

- **May/May not**—The Brits use the conditional a lot more than Americans. While "may" conveys the same meaning of being allowed to do something without its being mandatory, you will sometimes hear "may not" used in situations where you *absolutely cannot* do something under any circumstances. This is most common in written instructions (e.g., about purchase refunds, application procedures, etc.), so make sure you read things carefully.

- **Momentarily**—This word, to the Brits, only means "for a fleeting moment"; if you tell someone that you'll be with them "momentarily," they will think they're in for a second of your attention and no more. It does not mean "in a moment," although this linguistic debate is on the increase in the UK, so you might be understood.

- **Neat**—The Brits don't use this word to mean "great," although they might understand an American's meaning. What will cause confusion is that in the UK, "neat" means "tidy" or "compact." If they said your kitchen was looking very neat, they would be complimenting you on how tidy it looked, rather than expressing admiration for your decor. A neat pile of clothes would refer to clothes that had probably been folded as opposed to flung all over the floor. "Neat" is also used when ordering liquor which is to be served without ice or water, e.g., a neat brandy.

- **Orient**—Although Americans understand both "orient" and "orientate" as verbs, Brits never use the former word, and they might not catch your meaning for a while.

- **Out of pocket**—Telling someone you'll be out of pocket next week will probably elicit the response, "How can you be so sure?" since the phrase in the UK means to be out of money, and would never be used to mean out of circulation or unavailable, as it sometimes is in the States.

- **Quite**—Beware: this word has almost the opposite meaning in the two countries. In the UK, using "quite" to describe something means only that it was okay. Example: "The concert was quite good" means that the person speaking was mildly disappointed in it. Be careful when using this word as it could convey the opposite of what you mean. If your dinner host asks how you liked the Beef Wellington, the response, "Quite good, thank you," is not recommended.

- **Route**—Always pronounced "root." If you pronounce it "rowt," Brits may either not follow your meaning or will think you mean an "utter defeat" (*OED* definition). Incidentally, the phrase "en route" is pronounced more closely to the French pronunciation, "on root." If you say "en rowt," as most Americans do, you may not be understood.

- **Smart**—A smart American is someone who aced math (as they say) or who has done very well in life. However, a smart Brit would be someone who is always very nicely dressed. So, when praising someone for their colossal intelligence, avoid the word "smart" as the Brits will at least initially think you're pausing to admire that person's attire!

- **Tick off**—In the UK, this phrase has two meanings—and neither is the American meaning of making someone angry. If a person gets ticked off in the UK, he or she has been reprimanded. This is often referred to as giving or receiving a "good ticking off." The second meaning is to check something off a list—"Shall I tick that one off, then?" A "tick mark" in your schoolbook means that whatever you wrote met the approval of the teacher.

- **Vet** (the noun)—The term "vet" only ever refers to an animal doctor. If you're talking about the other kind of vet, say "ex-Army," "ex-Navy," etc. If you hear a reference to Chelsea Pensioners, they are the oldest surviving war veterans and don bright red uniforms on Poppy Day (Remembrance Day).

- **Vet** (the verb)—The Brits quite often use the verb "to vet" something, to mean to check something over. If you say you're having a party, some wit might say, "Let's vet the guest list to make sure it'll be good." More typically, someone might vet applications for a job, meaning to screen them for interviews.

- **To visit**—"To visit" in the UK only means that you physically go to visit a person or a national monument. It would never be used to sit and chat, as in "Come over here and visit with me." The response would be, "What are we visiting?" It is quite common to "revisit" a subject in conversation, however.

- **To "wash up"**—In the UK this means to do the dishes. If you're meaning to say that you need to clean yourself up in any way, either say just that or use phrases such as "freshen up" or "use the bathroom"—which of course would not mean that you needed the loo! While on the subject of doing the dishes, most British sinks have built-in draining boards and the Brits use them. There is generally no need to wash then rinse dishes under cold running water; indeed this practice has a tendancy to irritate Brits, who much prefer to either leave things to drip dry or to dry them properly with a tea towel.

- **Yanks**—Most Brits call all Americans "Yanks" and are not aware of the differences between the North and the South. No offense at all is intended.

YET MORE CONFUSING THINGS

Spelling and Grammar Notes

You'll become almost immediately familiar with spelling differences such as color/colour, theater/theatre, and neighbor/neighbour. In general, these don't cause problems because the pronunciation and meaning stays the same; and if a Brit pretends not to understand such words when written down, he or she is either thick or just being awkward. There are, however, a few less well appreciated differences that could skew your meaning, or worse, bring forth yet another snort of derision from the nearest Brit.

- Certain regional American pronunciations might draw blank looks from Brits, such as the way many Americans say "mirror" and "error." In the UK, these words have two distinct syllables, so the American pronunciations often sound like "meer" and "air" to them.
- Other pronunciations will merely start up a new topic of conversation. Examples include "miniature"—in the UK the middle "i" is silent; aluminum becomes "aluminium" (with an extra syllable); behoove becomes "behove"; and the word "herb" has an audible "h."
- Quotation marks are called "inverted commas"; a period is a "full stop," and parentheses are known as "brackets."

Clocks and Calendars

When making an appointment with a Brit, you might hear "half four" or even "four-thirty (pause) five." The former would mean four-thirty, and the latter means between four-thirty and five o'clock, rather than four-thirty-five. Although Brits will definitely understand the more common American habit of saying "four-fifteen," etc., they do not normally use it themselves—hence four-fifteen is usually phrased as "a quarter past four." Additionally, when saying forty-five minutes past the hour, they are more likely to say "a quarter *to*" the hour (not "a quarter *of*").

Calendar dates are, quite frankly, a disaster waiting to happen. Brits *always* write the day number followed by the month, and most would not even know that Americans do it the other way round. When in doubt (as you will be after several months of doing this), write the month out in full and you'll avoid a few calamities.

You'll probably hear references to "British Summertime" somewhere around March. This, I admit, sounds like an oxymoron, but is actually a reference to the clocks going forward an hour, as in the States. In the UK, this is done a week earlier than when the U.S. goes over to Daylight Savings Time. The Brits, by the way, won't know what you're talking about if you say Daylight Savings Time. In the fall the clocks go back at the same time, and the British refer to this as GMT, or Greenwich Mean Time.

And finally, a word of warning—Mother's Day occurs in March in the UK and Father's Day, although in June, is not always the same date. Forewarned is forearmed, as they say.

RESOURCES

www.usingenglish.com—a great Web site to teach the English language to foreigners; also gives swear words, idioms, and has a search tool

www.askoxford.com—the online version of the *Concise Oxford English Dictionary*

http://dictionary.cambridge.org—the online version of the Cambridge University dictionary

5

Out and About

APART FROM a few of the older East Coast cities in America, the United Kingdom and the United States just "look" different—and I'm not referring to the gray skies and drizzle. Pretty much wherever you are in the UK, you know you're not in the States (and vice versa). A few things are extremely obvious, like the lack of blue mailboxes, no overhanging traffic lights or twenty-foot-high billboards. (The UK has billboards but they are not usually erected along motorways.) The houses tend to look smaller and closer together. The Dursleys' house in the Harry Potter movies is pretty typical of a new housing development in the UK. Watch BBC America's home improvement shows for a sneak preview of what to expect.

Faced with all this new stuff, it's easy to feel overwhelmed getting from A to B, or having to do the simplest of errands. Do the ATMs (called "cash point machines") look the same? What is a bridleway? Fear not, I'm here to give you a head start.

- Despite the fact that the English singer Petula Clark sang about "downtown," it actually doesn't exist in British cities. If you ask the natives how to get downtown, they'll probably ask you where that is! You'll need to say either that you want to go "into town" or to the town center. When talking about London, there really is no town center as it's such a large city with many different areas. (By the way, since it's a major international city, it's never referred to as "London Town"). Similarly, you won't find a Main Street, but you will come across the High Street in every city, town, and village. You'll also hear references to High Street retailers, which basically means the chain stores that are found in nearly every city and town shopping area.

- Many cities in the UK are very old, and the town centers consist of extremely narrow streets. For this reason, many have been paved and are now pedestrian-only shopping areas. This, coupled with the ever popular one-way traffic systems, makes driving around these towns and cities a nightmare until you memorize the route. When obtaining directions to city locations, make sure you listen carefully— a wrong turn or a missed light could get you stuck in the one-way system, rerouted about sixty miles, and eventually placed on the Missing Persons list.

- The streets are paved with tarmac, referred to as "tar." Although it's the same stuff, the Brits don't call it blacktop or asphalt. Incidentally (and this could save a life or two), the Brits refer to the sidewalk as the pavement, and not the road itself. If you are directed to stand on the pavement, don't go to the middle of the road!

- Let's talk about the traffic for a second: While you will rarely see LA-type congestion (mainly because it's usually not that sunny), the UK can become fairly congested from time to time. Actually, I lie—the M25 is generally regarded as drivers' hell and to be avoided at all costs, especially between 6 a.m.–11 a.m. and 1 p.m.–8 p.m. If you plan to drive around London, you must pay the daily congestion charge or face a fine. You can pay this ahead of time or up until midnight of the day you drove into London (although drivers paying between 10 p.m. and midnight of that day pay an additional fee). Payment can be made online, at gas stations and stores where you see the "C" logo, by telephone, or by mail.

When you pay, your car license plate (vehicle number plate) is photographed and entered into a database. Cars entering the Congestion Zone are similarly logged and a comparison made between those who pay and those who do not. You will not receive a ticket when paying. You will know when you are entering the Congestion Zone as there are large red "C" signs everywhere (almost like the Chicago Cubs logo, only red). The Congestion Charge is in effect Monday through Friday (public holidays excluded), from 7 a.m. until 6.30 p.m. Most people don't take their cars into central London anyway, as it's usually quicker either to walk, take the Tube, or hop on a bus. Since taxis are still allowed to drive around London, anyone who has not taken a taxi there for several years will marvel at the comparative distance that can now be covered in less than five minutes.

- Speaking of public transport—Despite the fact that the Brits complain loudly and frequently about their public transport system, many Americans will be moderately impressed. You can pretty much get a train or a bus to any corner of the country. (*When* it will come is another matter entirely.)

Unlike many of their American counterparts, British city buses don't just go north/south or east/west. This is partly because nothing is built on a grid system, and partly to maximize the areas served. If you look at a bus route (pronounced "root"), for example, it will appear to amble aimlessly, so be patient; you will get to your destination, but the route will be circuitous. I have been particularly impressed in recent years by a digital sign that is now a feature of many bus shelters around the country. These signs give you the estimated arrival times of the buses scheduled to stop there. The vote is still out as to their usefulness, as the one near my mother's house rarely even has the correct bus number up! (A "bus shelter," incidentally, is a tempered glass or Plexiglas construction, without doors, giving shelter from the driving rain and howling winds to those awaiting the next bus.)

Trains are a bit more direct, but unless you're on a fast commuter train or an intercity express, they also tend to rumble along. When traveling by train, you can often buy your ticket ahead of time either at the station or online. Make sure you have a ticket *before* you board as ticket inspectors can fine you on the spot for traveling without first paying. Don't throw away your ticket when you get off the train, as it is usually required to get out of the station.

Unfortunately, transport strikes are fairly frequent in the UK, and can bring whole cities to their knees. National strikes are less common than regional ones, but also happen, usually at the busiest times of the year.

• You can also travel quite well using taxis in the UK, although the system is not quite the same as in the States. There are two different types of taxis, with a different set of rules governing each. The black cab, also known as a hackney carriage, is famed in London and can also be found in many of the larger cities around the country. In London, and many other cities, these are the only taxis that can legally "ply for hire," or be hailed off the street. If they are empty and available for hire, they will have a lit up sign on the top of the car and you can stick your hand out as you would anywhere. In addition, these cabs can be found outside major train stations, airports, and various city center locations. They are not usually found in more rural areas. The advantage of taking a black cab in London is that these drivers study for years before obtaining their license and therefore know every street within a six mile radius of Charing Cross. If you're not in the mood, the downside is that these chirpy drivers never stop talking and you'll know their life history and political views before you've traveled a half mile.

The other type of taxi is generally known as a mini cab. These cabs must be booked ahead of time either by phoning the company office or booking online. They are not allowed to drive around the streets looking for customers so if you attempt to hail one, it will probably drive straight on. These mini cabs look more like American cabs although they don't have a light on top, and sometimes don't even have company advertising on the exterior. All drivers must have an operator's license or temporary permit, as determined by the local city council. If you book one of the cabs by phone, the booking person can usually give you a price quote for your ride, which the driver should honor. In many large cities in the UK you'll find these cabs at various stands dotted around, however, there are often very long lines late at night. If you know when you'll be taking your return journey, mini cab companies will let you book a cab to come and pick you up from wherever you state. You should be warned however, that if you're late for the taxi, there are plenty of people who'll be more than ready to take your place, and the driver might not hesitate to take another paying customer.

- The bad news is that towns, villages, and cities rarely follow the grid system, so abandon all hope of intelligent guess-work when you're traveling around. Many places are extremely old and grew up in seemingly random fashion. Even new housing developments ignore the opportunity to make it easy to find people, and have cul-de-sacs (dead ends) everywhere, curving streets and identical houses. People have been known to wander for hours trying to visit friends in such places. With these types of layouts, directions are doomed before you even attempt them: "Well, the street sort of curves round to the right but it's not strictly a noticeable angle" has you nervously wondering whether you've actually taken that curve already and missed a vital clue. I wish people who live in such developments would hoist a flag when expecting visitors!

  For these reasons, the Brits tend to ignore the compass when giving you directions. People generally will tell you to "take a right" at certain spots rather than going north, south, etc. When you are asking for or giving directions, remember that mentioning any points on a compass will introduce distraction to an already complicated mission. You need to be on the lookout for pubs and churches. There are tons of them everywhere and they serve as great landmarks.

- Finding people's houses can also be a nightmare because of the tendency to have Acacia Avenue, Street, Close, Crescent, and Drive all in the same town, but not necessarily anywhere close to each other. When sending mail to someone, don't assume they live on Acacia *Street* and don't just write "Acacia." You must be very specific about the nomenclature—Street, Gardens, Avenue, Drive, Close, whatever. Also, if you're driving, don't assume everything is a street or avenue—listen carefully for the address. If you're taking a cab, make sure you have the *exact* address or you'll be in for a lecture from the driver.

  Be warned, also, that some houses you visit may have very strange addresses—or no number. Although quaint-sounding, these houses are often extremely tedious to find as the house name is either hidden by peeling paint on the sign, engulfed by a giant rhododendron, or simply not there at all. If you're given just a house name as the address, either ask what the house looks like or for some other visual clue should you get lost. Having said that, I recently visited a friend's new house, which supposedly had a "big white rock" at the end of the driveway. After three drive-bys, I finally realized she was talking about the grayish stone that couldn't have been more than a foot in diameter.

- You'll notice a distinct lack of yellow school buses. For the most part, children make their own way to school by being driven, walking, or taking regular public transport. Public transport buses vary in color throughout the land, depending on the city you're in and the particular company running that service. Even where special buses are provided exclusively to transport kids to and from school, they are not a uniform size, shape, or color. You'll also notice far fewer joggers in the UK, and definitely fewer in-line skaters and anything else on wheels except cars. Since most places (except remote country lanes) have sidewalks, however, it's usually good jogging terrain, as long as you take a rain slicker.

- Although the UK is quite a small country, there's plenty of opportunity to get out into what Brits call "the country-side." Every major city has quick and easy access to beautiful areas, although from London it might take you a little longer to get there. Some of the land is owned by the National Trust (or the Scottish Trust), along with many wonderful stately homes and museums. Both trusts are registered charities and were set up to buy property to preserve—and in many cases restore—for future generations. If you're planning to visit a number of their sites, you can purchase a Trust membership card, which then gives you free admission and parking to all their properties. You can save huge amounts of valuable time and money by doing this. Visit the Web sites for more information.

If you're going to be in the UK during the summer, bear in mind that the Brits love their National Trust properties and visit them often, thus ensuring long lines to get into the most popular spots, as well as packed parking lots (car parks). This popularity also means that the time it takes to drive to your chosen beauty spot might be longer than you expect. Many country tourist attractions are accessed by narrow roads and long, winding driveways. You can spend a long time just sitting in your car waiting to go through the entrance.

If you're planning to do a lot of driving in the UK, first of all, read the relevant chapter in this book (chapter 6).

Second, don't plan your itinerary based solely on miles to be covered. You also need to take into consideration which roads will get you there. A "B" road will certainly be the more scenic, but if you get stuck behind a tractor or a herd of cows, it could literally double your travel time.

- There are a lot of public restrooms dotted about the UK, both indoors (e.g., shopping centers) and outdoors (e.g., parks). These loos range from spotlessly clean to downright disgusting so check them out before allowing your children to use them. Since there's generally no gap between the floor and the door, if your child gets locked in a cubicle, you could be in trouble.

- Although the weather's usually a bit "iffy," as they say, the UK has plenty of outside sports and activities. In recent years a number of holiday centers (such as Center Parcs) have sprung up where you can take various lessons or just enjoy outdoor activities ranging from canoeing to horse riding and hiking. There are also many footpaths where you can safely ramble around the countryside without getting too lost or trespassing on anyone's property. The issue of trespassing is sometimes a thorny one, so make sure you follow the signs when walking. Anyone can use a public footpath; a "permissive" footpath, although rather salacious-sounding, basically means that the land is privately owned but the public is allowed to walk through. Bridleways are also open to the public and to horse riders and cyclists. The Ramblers' Association has a great Web site explaining all of this.

- Talking about the weather—the UK has a fairly mild climate, but it is extremely unpredictable. (A word here: The Brits are well aware that their weather is not always what one would want. There's usually no need to remind them of this by complaining about gray skies or cool summers.) Although umbrellas (often called brollies) are not always easy to carry about, especially when hiking, it is advisable to take some sort of waterproof outer layer. Also, if you're visiting in the summer, don't assume that you'll only need light cotton clothing. I have had to purchase fleeces for my kids in the middle of July or August on many occasions.

- England, Northern Ireland, Scotland, and Wales all have their own Tourism Boards, giving a wealth of information on every aspect of each country. There are also Tourism Boards for many individual counties, as well as a separate board for London. In most cities you'll find a Tourist Information Office, and all the boards have their own Web sites. They are worth checking out as you not only learn about where you're going, but often can obtain discount fares and other bargains.

BRITISH WORDS THAT MIGHT REQUIRE TRANSLATION

The A to Z (pronounced "Zed") *n*—street map (you can get them for every city)

Brolly *n*—umbrella

City center *n*—downtown

Common *n*—village green or heathland

Cul-de-sac *n*—dead end

Double decker *n*—two-level bus

Pavement *n*—sidewalk

Semi, or semi-detached *n*—duplex

Subway *n*—underpass

Tube *n* (in London)—subway; also called the Underground

AMERICAN WORDS THAT THE BRITS DON'T SHARE

Downtown—city center

Duplex—most commonly, a semi-detached

Strip malls—shopping centers

Subway—Tube (in London) or Underground train

RESOURCES

www.nationalrail.co.uk—National Rail's Web site, where you can check schedules, buy tickets, and plan journeys

www.nationaltrust.org.uk—The National Trust Web site (England, Wales, and N. Ireland)

www.nts.org.uk—The National Trust for Scotland Web site

www.visitscotland.com—Official site of Scotland's National Tourism Board

www.tourism.wales.gov.uk—Official site of the Welsh Tourism Board

www.discovernorthernireland.com—Official site of Northern Ireland's Tourism Board

www.londontouristboard.com—London's official Tourism Board site

www.visitbritain.com—Official UK Tourism Board site

www.ramblers.org.uk—The Ramblers' Association Web site

www.tfl.gov.uk—Transport for London's Web site

www.cclondon.com—Transport for London Congestion Charge information

www.paypoint.co.uk—Paypoint Web site, giving exact locations of where to pay the London Congestion Charge

www.traintaxi.com—a great Web site that tells you which rail stations have taxi ranks outside, and how to get from smaller rail stations to your destination

6

Drive Time

APART FROM THE FACT that it happens on the other side of the road, driving in the UK is generally not too bad, although the larger cities suffer the typical traffic problems of any big city. I find that in most instances, British drivers let me cut into the traffic lanes (as long as I'm "indicating" and smiling politely), and are neither overly aggressive nor seriously dangerous. Happily, there are far fewer octogenarians driving around at 15mph.

I would strongly advise acquainting yourself with British road rules and signs before getting behind the wheel, as ignorance of even the basics could cost a life. Grab a copy of the *Highway Code,* which you'll find online, as well as in soft cover throughout the UK.

- You must obtain a British driving license within one year of arriving in the UK.

    Getting a license requires a written and actual driving

test, which, I hate to say, is on a par with a root canal. (Apparently there's a big PR campaign under way to soften the image of the whole ordeal.) There have been major changes in recent years so make sure that any kindly Brit who's guiding you through the process actually has a clue. The test is divided into three parts: Thirty-five multiple-choice questions, followed by a "hazard perception skills" test—not as scary as it sounds. You have to pass these two tests at the same sitting, and then take the actual driving test, which will probably require some lessons from a qualified instructor. According to my American friends who have lived through this ordeal, the experienced U.S. driver can expect to need about three or four lessons; the newer driver may require up to ten. These lessons are expensive but necessary, as even slight variations from driving protocol can fail you. For example, most driving instructors will tell you to angle your rearview mirror so that you actually have to move your head slightly to see behind you. This will allow the examiner to see that you are using this mirror at regular intervals. You are also expected to use the parking brake (handbrake) almost every time you stop for more than a few seconds.

You can find out all you need to know (including an instructor) through the government's Web site (below), and even book your test there. Your driving test will take about 40 minutes and there is a fee. Driving examiners are not regarded for their sense of humor while testing drivers, so the whole experience is usually quite stressful. Many people fail the first time and this carries no stigma at all.

While learning to drive, any vehicle driven by the learner must display red "L" plates. When the learner is not driving the car, those "L" plates are supposed to be removed. Before getting behind the wheel or taking any part of the test, learners must first obtain a "provisional driving license"; they cannot drive unaccompanied, and must be accompanied by a driver who has been qualified for at least three years and is over the age of twenty-one. This means that your teenager, who is learning to drive, can't be accompanied by the friend who passed the test last week. Learner drivers are not allowed on freeways (motorways) so many newly qualified drivers take "motorway driving" lessons after their test. There are now green "L" plates for those who have just passed their test, but these are not mandatory. High schools typically do not offer "driver's ed." The minimum age for driving or learning to drive is seventeen.

Far fewer cars in the UK are automatic. If you pass your test driving an automatic, you are not authorized to drive a stick shift (or "manual") car in the UK. Most students use their instructor's car for the test, thus ensuring that it is up to scratch (and I think because the examiners must prefer the comfort of having a foot brake on their side also).

- If you plan to drive a motorcycle or a moped you will also be required to obtain a provisional license, pass a driving test, and then apply for a full license. You must be sixteen to ride a moped and seventeen for a motorcycle.

- Your car must have a tax disk (displayed at all times) for a period of six or twelve months. This can be purchased at your local Post Office, with proof of ownership, MOT certification if required (see p. 60), and driving license. Tax disks are not transferable from one car to another, and failure to display one results in a hefty fine.

- Check to see whether your American auto insurance covers you overseas. In many cases it won't, and you should probably buy coverage once you arrive in the UK.

- Because Brits drive on the left, I would *not* recommend getting off a transatlantic flight and straight into the driver's seat when visiting the UK, especially if you've never done it before. Give yourself at least 24 hours to acclimate (which is called "acclimatize" by the way) to the flow of traffic and it'll seem much less daunting. Fortunately, the foot pedals are in the same position, and as the steering wheel is now on the right, you still have to be situated in the middle of the road when driving. The most difficult times for me are usually when there is no other traffic on the road to keep me straight! I have had fleeting moments of panic in which I think I'm driving on the wrong side, or perhaps driving down a one-way street the wrong way. Less dangerous, and more entertaining, will be your attempts to get into the car (walking toward the wrong door) and fasten your seatbelt (sticking your hand into your passenger's face). Some friends have resorted to wearing a glove on one hand only, to remind them of the correct side of the road.

- Speed limits. The speed limit on freeways (motorways) is 70 mph; it is not advisable to go much faster as enforcement differs widely throughout the UK, and in recent years, speed cameras have been introduced. Now, speeding motorists are caught in the act on camera, and then sent a fine and demand for payment. Rumor has it that only about 20 percent of these cameras are operating at any one time, but since you never know which ones, it's better to slow down when you see the warning road sign. In the last year or so there has been an undercurrent of revolt by the British driving public as there seem to be so many speed cameras around. In 2004, a small brewing company in the North-east produced a new beer, which they named "Highway Robbery," in protest. Every batch sold out immediately.

Speeding offenses rack up points on your license, which not only increase your insurance premiums but also eventually lead to the license being suspended. I know of a handful of close friends and family who have already been nailed by speed cameras. New drivers who rack up six points or more in the first two years lose their license and have to re-sit the driving test! If caught speeding, going through a red light, driving carelessly, driving without insurance, or failing to stop after an accident, you will receive between three and ten points. Your license will be suspended when you reach twelve points, and be warned, this total can be achieved surprisingly quickly.

- Similarly, UK drivers do not tend to break road and driving laws such as going through red or orange (amber) lights, parking where it is illegal, etc., as the fines are usually high. There is also the dreaded "clamp" (similar to the boot or Denver Boot), which is a pain in the neck to get unlocked, and extremely expensive. When in doubt, stick to 70mph on freeways and 30mph in built-up areas, obey all road signs, and *don't* park illegally.

- When driving on any multi-lane road, you can only overtake on the right side (the outside lane). *Never* attempt to disobey this rule as no one will be expecting you to come up on the wrong side, and the higher road speeds in the UK almost guarantee fatal injury.

- You may not turn on a red light *under any circumstance*

whatsoever, other than a green filter arrow. Nor should you go through an orange (amber) light. If you are trying to turn against the traffic at traffic lights, you must not enter the junction and sit there. You are supposed to stay at the light and wait until you can make the turn. (There is no grace period in which to turn after a light has changed to orange or red.) Such restricted areas are usually marked with a yellow grid or rectangle on the road surface.

- If you encounter malfunctioning lights at an intersection, never, ever attempt the four-way stop procedure. It does not exist in the UK and you are likely to get yourself killed. General chaos will ensue until a traffic warden from the next block or village is wheeled in to help.

- Although parking in England—and particularly in London—is usually tight, it is not acceptable to bump other cars when attempting to squeeze into a space. Basically, if you can't get the car in without hitting another car—it doesn't fit! Plus you run the risk of setting off someone's car alarm, which has happened to me a few times. When parking, the Brits leave the car in neutral with the parking brake (handbrake) on. If you borrow someone's car, for heaven's sake don't leave it in gear when you return it, or the owner will kangaroo straight through the garden wall next time the engine's turned on.

- A word about the parking meters—you are not supposed to refill your meter when the money runs out. You should drive off and come back, as if you've never been there. "Yeah, right," I hear you say. This is particularly vexing in heavily trafficked areas when you know the spot won't be there when you return. Unfortunately, if you're caught "feeding the meter," there's usually a fine to pay.

- The street parking in England will cause you a moment's panic now and then. On most two-way streets, cars can park facing either direction. From time to time, I've found myself driving down a street in which all the parked cars were facing me. As long as you pay attention to any signs before you enter a street, you should be okay.

- British police quite often have less to do than in the United States, so if you're followed by a police car, drive as well as you can and expect to be pulled over for something. Police can and do stop and search cars, especially late at night. Make sure you always have roadworthy tires (spelled "tyres") in your vehicle, including a spare. Tires should have a tread depth of at least 1 mm, across three quarters of the breadth of the tire and all around the circumference. (See your *Highway Code* for details.) Similarly, never drive with a faulty light or anything hanging off your car, as you'll almost definitely be pulled over.

- Police do not generally write parking tickets; for that you'll have to look out for the ever present traffic warden. He or she wears a uniform and a peaked hat with a yellow band. Pleading ignorance as a foreigner will probably not work, but it may be worth a try. Just don't pick a fight or you'll end up in more trouble; their reputation is only slightly less frightening than that of driving examiners, and as far as I know, they are making no effort to soften their image.

- Drink/driving regulations are much more stringently adhered to and enforced. It is worth remembering that as in the United States, drinking and driving in the UK is generally not considered clever or funny by anyone. The culture has become quite intolerant of such behavior, and people either use public transport or don't drink when they have to drive their car. You will not simply be cautioned if found over the limit; you will receive a minimum one-year ban and possibly a large fine, even for your first offense. Your insurance premiums will also increase significantly. The legal limit is 0.08 mg, which is more stringent than in some U.S. states. The abbreviations DUI and DWI mean nothing in the UK. The phrases used are "drink/driving" and "over the limit"; the legal charge is "drunk in charge of . . ." and you can also be caught drunk in charge of a bicycle!

- It is an offense to drive while using a handheld phone or similar device; this law also applies to drivers waiting at lights or sitting in stationary traffic.

- Be prepared for some very high gas (petrol) prices in the UK. Obviously the dollar-to-pound exchange rate has some impact, but in recent years, gas prices in the UK have been at least double those in the States. Car prices are also a lot higher than most U.S. equivalents, but you can negotiate with the dealer over the price.

- In addition to the driver and front passenger, it is now an offense in the UK for rear passengers to travel without using seatbelts. Again, this tends to be strictly adhered to and you may be stopped for ignoring this rule. The person fined will be the person not wearing the seatbelt, rather than the driver.

- If you're a motorcycle rider, be warned, nowhere in the UK is it permitted to forget your crash helmet.

- Bicycles also have their own rules & regulations. If you ride a bicycle at night, it must have a working front white light, a back red light, and a red reflector. Always lock or chain up your bike as bike theft is very common.

- If you own a car that is more than three years old, it must be tested according to the Ministry of Transport (MOT) standards. This test can be done at any repair shop (called a "garage") which is MOT-authorized; without it, you will not be able to purchase the mandatory car tax sticker or insure your car. Failure to display an up-to-date tax disk will result in a fine; this includes stationary vehicles parked on the street outside your house.

- Be aware of "Zebra crossings." You'll recognize them because of the huge black and white stripes painted across the road. (Think Beatles—*Abbey Road.*) They are usually flanked by two pillars with a yellow ball at the top, called Belisha Beacons. As soon as pedestrians set foot on the road, they have the right of way on these crossings and will assume that all cars will stop. The other type of pedestrian crossing (often called a Pelican crossing) looks more like regular traffic lights in the middle of the road. There is no clearly marked crossing, but the road on either side usually has jagged markings at the curbside. When a pedestrian wishes to cross, he or she presses the button. The lights will change and a loud beeping sound occurs (for the deaf) to let them cross. You may not go through these lights when red, even if no one is around. When the lights flash, drivers may proceed if no pedestrians are waiting to cross.

Although there are no laws against jay-walking in the UK (indeed, the term is not used), pedestrians walking out into the road other than on a crossing could be hit by the first vehicle that comes along. Drivers often drive at higher speeds than in the United States and will not be expecting anyone to step out into the road or walk between the cars.

- Roundabouts (traffic circles) are everywhere in the UK, and it's basically survival of the most daring! You must give way (yield) to vehicles coming from the right at all roundabouts. Mercifully, at the busiest roundabouts, traffic lights have been installed to give drivers a snowflake's chance of actually making it round. After remembering to drive around in clockwise fashion, the main rule is that if you're taking the first or second exit off the roundabout, you should stay in the *outside* lane. If you need to drive all the way round, you should immediately make for the *inside* lane and move to the outside as you approach your exit. You will also encounter "mini" roundabouts. They look like small white mounds in the road, but should be treated the same as regular roundabouts, i.e., don't drive over them! Another great reason not to get straight behind the wheel when landing at Heathrow Airport is the number of confusing roundabouts you'll encounter almost immediately.

- An "M" road—as in the M1, M4, M5—means that it's a freeway (motorway); an "A" road is a divided highway (dual carriageway); and a "B" road can be anything from a country lane to a fairly decent road. If you can get to your destination using motorways and/or A roads, do so unless you want the scenic advantages of B roads. Yes, the B roads are usually more picturesque, but hours spent trundling along behind an ancient piece of farm equipment will probably change your strategy before too long.

Incidentally, if you're planning to cover two thirds of the country in less than 24 hours (as many Americans seem to do), don't gauge your travel itinerary by drawing straight lines on a map. Many times you won't be able to drive as the crow flies, so careful planning is essential. Should you need to take a B road, or go through any major city, I would advise you to add at least an hour or two to your travel time. It is worth talking to someone who knows the roads before completing your itinerary, as there are many "black spots" to be avoided, such as the M25, which encircles the greater London area and is jammed almost 24/7.

- If you decide to take a British car over to the Continent for an excursion, exercise extreme caution. Yes, they all drive on the "correct" side of the road, as in the States, but don't forget you're sitting on the other side of the car. It will be very difficult to pass a car, as you won't be able to see round it. Any junctions should be approached with care, as you'll be turning on the outside rather than the inside of the road. Personally, I would rent a car *after* arriving on the mainland.

- There are and always have been different names for similar cars in the UK and the United States. The "Bug" is generally known as the "Beetle" over there, and a "Rabbit" is a "Golf." A Mercedes is often called a Merc, rather than a Benz, and a BMW is not always known as a Beamer. Instead of referring to something as the "Cadillac" of whatever, the Brits will use the term "Rolls-Royce." Same difference.

- By the way, the Brits pronounce the Jaguar as "Jag-you-ar" and a Peugot as "Pur-jo"—except as an American, you'd roll the "r" sound, which they don't do. "Fiat" has a flatter "a," as in "flat."

BRITISH WORDS THAT MIGHT REQUIRE TRANSLATION

AA—Automobile Association (equivalent of the AAA)

Aerial *n*—antenna

Amber light *n*—orange light

Articulated lorry *n*—trailer truck

"B" road *n*—more rural road, usually single-lane

Banger *n*—old car (also a sausage)

Belisha Beacon *n*—pole with orange ball on top, flanking a "Zebra crossing"

Bollard *n*—sturdy metal post used to stop cars driving onto pedestrianized areas

Bonnet *n*—hood

Boot *n*—trunk

Bump start *v*—to start a manual car by popping the clutch

Bumper *n*—fender

Car park *n*—parking lot

Caravan *n*—trailer; RV

Caravan site *n*—trailer park (permanent residence at one of these is not common)

Cats' eyes *n*—road reflectors

Central reservation *n*—median

Clamp *n*—boot, Denver Boot

Crash *n*—wreck

Double yellow-lined area—a no parking area

Dual carriageway ("A" road) *n*—divided highway

Estate car *n*—station wagon

Flyover *n*—overpass

Four-wheel drive *n*—SUV

Garage *n*—garage, gas station, body shop

Gear/manual car—car with stick shift

Gear box *n*—transmission

Give way—yield

Handbrake *n*—parking brake

Indicators *n*—turn signals

Juggernaut *n*—18-wheeler

Kerb *n*—curb

Lollipop man/lady *n*—school crossing guard

Lorry *n*—truck

"M" road; motorway *n*—freeway

Multi-storey (car park) *n*—multi-level parking lot

Number plate *n*—license plate

Overtake *v*—to pass

Pavement *n*—sidewalk

Pedestrian crossing *n*—crosswalk

Petrol *n*—gas

Petrol station/garage *n*—gas station

Prang *v*—to have a minor collision with something

RAC—Royal Automobile Company (equivalent of the AAA)

Registration number *n*—license number

Reverse lights *n*—backup lights

Saloon *n*—sedan

Silencer *n*—muffler

Sleeping policeman *n*—speed bump

Ticking over *v*—idling

Traffic warden *n*—traffic cop who writes tickets and directs
traffic

Van *n*—small truck

Windscreen *n*—windshield

Write-off *n*—totaled car

Zebra crossing—a crosswalk with huge black and white stripes on the road. Cars *must* stop for pedestrians waiting to cross

AMERICAN WORDS THAT THE BRITS DON'T SHARE

Backup lights—reverse lights
Boot (Denver)—clamp
Curb—kerb
Divided highway—dual carriageway
Fender—bumper
Fender bender—the term is not used
Freeway—motorway
Hood—bonnet
Gaper delay—the term is not used
Gas—petrol
Gas/filling station—garage, service station, petrol station
Grease monkey—mechanic
License number—Registration number
License plate—number plate
Muffler—silencer
Orange light—amber light
Parking brake—handbrake
Parking lot—car park
Pavement—road
Rubber necking—the term is not used
RV—caravan
Sedan—saloon
Sidewalk—pavement

Speed bump—sleeping policeman
Station wagon—estate car
Stick shift—gear or manual (car)
Traffic cop—traffic warden
Trailer—caravan
Trailer park—caravan site
Turn signals—indicators
Truck—lorry, van
Trunk—boot
Windscreen—windshield

RESOURCES

www.dvla.gov.uk—Driving and Vehicle Licensing Agency's Web site
www.dsa.gov.uk—Driving Standards Agency: information about the driving tests
www.tso-online.co.uk—The Stationery Office (where you can order the *Highway Code*)
www.theaa.co.uk—Automobile Association's Web site
www.rac.co.uk—Royal Automobile Association's Web site

7

Home, Sweet Home

MOST AMERICANS tend to think that British houses are small; most British houses are in fact smaller than the average American house. They usually have distinct rooms, with doors rather than archways, although open-plan styles are becoming more popular.

Typically, you'll walk straight into a hallway, no matter how small. (Most Brits, including myself, have an inbuilt aversion to opening the front door and walking straight into the living room.) In many cases the hallway is there to keep the cold out of the living room, and to keep noise from traveling upstairs. The stairways are often not as high or as wide as in the States (as my husband, at six feet four, can attest), especially in structures from the nineteenth century and before. If you're lucky enough to visit a house, pub, or hotel from about the sixteenth century, the doors are often so small that even women have to stoop to enter. A word here—complaining loudly every time you hit your head on an original Tudor beam will generally be looked on as uncouth!

I'm giving you this information so that you don't walk into someone's house and immediately start marveling at how small or "quaint" certain things are. This is usually met with frosty looks and only serves to maintain yet another stereotype that Americans think their stuff is always bigger and better.

Just so you're prepared, a few other gems follow.

- Buying a house in the UK is a little different (surprise, surprise). You don't need an agent to buy a house (although you can hire them to help you), and if you want to sell one, you simply go along to one of the many "estate agent" offices you'll see. It's also okay to list your house with more than one estate agent. As in the States, you'll need a lawyer (solicitor) to do the conveyancing of the property (transfer ownership). The big thing to be wary of is "gazzump-ing (or gazumping)." No, it's not a hideous disease harbored in very old houses, but the practice of the seller accepting your offer and then accepting a higher offer at the very last minute. This is the scourge of house buying in much of the UK and is very common. It can even happen after the initial would-be purchaser has commissioned a survey, arranged financing, and sold his or her existing property. Once contracts have been exchanged between a buyer and seller, the sale is complete and gazzump-ing (or gazumping) can't happen. Since accepting an offer doesn't seal the deal, most purchasers ask the seller to take the property off the market and/or try to exchange contracts as quickly as possible.

  Gazzumping does not occur in Scotland because accepting an offer creates a legally binding arrangement.

(Obviously, this does not constitute legal advice on the matter and you should always consult a lawyer before buying or selling a house in the UK.)

- When you buy a house in the UK (and, as an American, you'll be allowed to), you shouldn't expect to see a place that is in move-in condition in terms of decor. Sellers assume that you will want to put your own "stamp" on the property, so very few of them waste money on new paint. You'll have to look past the garish wallpaper or outlandish faux finishes when viewing potential properties. In addition, far fewer people in the UK view a house and start thinking about tearing down walls or otherwise reconfiguring them, and the seller probably won't budge on price just because of changes you might feel should be made. If the house isn't configured the way a Brit wants, he or she will usually find another one and move straight in.

- Many people name their houses. Very old houses usually have a name because the street or road they are on didn't allocate numbers when the houses were first built. Newer homes are usually given names because the owners think it adds a certain prestige to the abode. The Royal Mail prefers that all named houses also have a number, but there's not a lot you can do if you move into a house that doesn't come with a number.

  When houses do have numbers, you'll usually find odd numbers on one side of a street and even on the other. Unfortunately, many of the newer housing developments have winding roads and the layout of the numbers will make you suspect a trick is being played on you.

- British houses are rarely air-conditioned and are heated by radiators, which are extremely hot to the touch and give off a surprising amount of heat. Some newer houses, which began life with forced air, are now converting back to radiators, as the Brits tend to prefer this. Windows don't have screens or storm windows, so you'll probably find flies buzzing in the summer. It doesn't bother anyone, and fly spray is sold everywhere!

- I would venture to say that the chief complaint among Americans staying in the UK is about the showers. Walk-in showers are not as common or as powerful as in the United States, and many Brits still prefer baths. Often, when you find a shower, it is a tub shower, the shower curtains are never quite long enough, and they have a tendency to stick to you as soon as the water starts running. If you're desperate for a really good shower, find a resident American. He or she will undoubtedly have ripped out the bathroom and rehabbed it "American style," or found the only house in the entire vicinity with a powerful shower.

- Many houses, especially with fewer than four bedrooms, do not have more than one full bathroom, although higher-end new houses are beginning to come with a bathroom for each bedroom, and loos dotted about all over the place (figuratively speaking). I was recently watching a show on BBC America, in which a couple is helped in their search for the perfect English country house. The couple in question didn't like one of the houses because it had "too many bathrooms" (one for each bedroom), and they thought it felt too much like a hotel! I have to add, though, that it was an old house, and numerous loos *did* seem a bit odd.

- Where owners of old homes have added loos or showers, you'll often find them in very strange places—under the stairs in the entry hall or in a tiny closet in the corner of a bedroom. If you're over six feet tall, there won't be a lot of room to maneuver.

- Bathrooms are often separate from the room containing the toilet, especially in older houses. If you ask for the bathroom, you might be shown only to a bathroom (with no toilet). "Restroom" is not a recognized word in the UK, and the word "toilet" refers to the room as well as the receptacle. Ask for the toilet, loo, ladies/men's room, or lavatory—these words are not offensive. The term "half bath" is not a word. Oh yes, the word "lavatory" in the UK refers to the toilet, as opposed to the hand basin. Don't have a heart attack to hear that someone "peed in the lavvy." A loo is never referred to as a "commode." The good news is that, since there's no requirement for low-flush toilets in the UK, they don't block up and overflow nearly as much.

- If the bathroom is accessed directly from a bedroom, it will be referred to as an "en suite" bathroom, both in homes and in hotels. Sometimes only the words "en suite" are used. In some bathrooms, while you might not find a toilet, you could encounter a bidet. Americans not accustomed to these have been known to use them as a toilet. Remember, if it doesn't have a tank or a handle to flush with, it probably isn't a toilet.

- In older houses, the hot and cold faucets (taps) are often mounted separately on sinks and baths, which bugs my husband as he says it's impossible to wash your hands or face in running water without incurring second-degree burns. (The idea, dearest, is that you're supposed to put the plug in and fill the sink.) While I acknowledge the burning potential, it also means that you can brush your teeth with nice cold water while waiting for the hot water to warm up.

Actually, since the hot water's coming out of a separate tap, it quite often comes out piping hot, so there *is* no waiting!

- Still on the subject of bathrooms, ask if it's okay to drink the water! In older houses it often comes from a tank in the attic, which is not chemically treated. These days it's usually okay to drink from the bathroom cold faucet, but I guarantee you'll find Brits who refuse to do this, although they won't be able to give you a valid reason.

- Many houses still do not have dishwashers, or waste disposal units in the sink—so pause before throwing anything in there. Most kitchen sinks have a great built-in draining board, but alas, not that handy little spray attachment you're used to.

- Washing machines and dryers are not as big as in the States, and are often located in the kitchen. The washing machines (usually front loaders), however, are very efficient and often require an advanced degree to work out the program required for your load. (Warning: If you're borrowing someone's house for your stay in the UK, make sure you get detailed instructions on how to use the machine. Every other appliance should be okay, but not the washer.) Dryers were often the type that simply extracted moisture from clothes (rather than blowing hot air around) but they have become more efficient recently—thank goodness. You will find that whenever there's a breezy day, people like to hang their washing outside. A common phrase when remarking on a sunny, breezy day (usually in jest) is "Lovely drying weather."

- Refrigerators, generally called "fridges," are nowhere near the size of American ones, so many families have a second fridge and perhaps even a chest freezer (commonly called a "deep" freezer), hidden away in the garage or the utility room. Check before having your jumbo fridge shipped over, or buying one in the United States fitted for British voltage, since it might not even fit into the designated space in your British kitchen. The cooking appliance is known as an oven, cooker, or stove, but the word "range" is rarely used unless you're referring to the enormous Aga-type ranges that are meant for farmhouses but can now be found in yuppie kitchens everywhere.

• Household appliances you won't easily find in the UK include waffle irons, stove-top griddles, big coolers, huge refrigerators, ice dispensers, three-way lamps, in-shower radios, steam-free shaving mirrors, mega outdoor grills, BBQ grills on an inside range, ceiling fans, window screens, good coffeemakers, electric skillets, snow blowers, leaf blowers, and top-loading washing machines. And most annoyingly, when you buy most household appliances, they don't always come with a plug on them.

Still on the topic of household appliances, you will often find British ones in very odd places—washing machines are invariably in or near the kitchen, while the dryer could literally be anywhere. Until recently, my mother's was in the garage, but when the new kitchen was fitted, a place was found in there for it. Many homes have a "utility room" where washers, dryers, and extra fridges or freezers stay. The hot water heater also can be almost anywhere in the house, but is usually kept in what's known as the "airing cupboard," which will be somewhere close to the bathroom. Airing cupboards are great for storing towels and sheets, which, when needed, are always lovely and warm, because of the hot water heater.

- Gardens are never called "yards," and are usually much more private. No matter how small the patch in front of a house, it is usually edged by a small wall, fence, or hedge. A "yard" in the UK refers to a concrete enclosure and was more typical of the tenement housing of the lower classes built during the Victorian era. Hence the word may open up a huge sociological can of worms with the Brits you encounter. Although decks are becoming more popular (being cheaper and easier to install), most outdoor "flooring" tends to be of the patio variety. "Crazy paving" usually refers to random shaped flagstones.

- Televisions don't quite reach the proportions of some in the United States, but this is only a matter of time. One thing that's available in the UK which you might not be familiar with is the text information on the "telly." *Ceefax*, available on the BBC, and *Teletext*, on Independent Television, is an information service available at the press of a button. Not only do you get TV-related information, but you can almost organize your life by it—new car pricing, vacation possibilities, government information—a veritable telly Internet. (See chapter 10 for more on the telly.)

- Closets the size of small rooms are a bit thin on the ground, especially in old houses. In newer houses, you'll get "fitted wardrobes," which are like built-ins in the States. In older houses, however, you'll get a square room with windows—hence the British fondness for wardrobes, and other free-standing furniture.

- Having trawled through scores of British bed manufacturer's Web sites, there doesn't seem to be much uniformity in the names given to different sized beds. The term "queen" is not often used for a double bed. If you will be staying in furnished accommodation but are required to take your own bed linen, ask for specific measurements as the U.S. and UK versions of "double" and "king" often differ.

- Household animals: Generally, the Brits have the same kind of pets as in the States, although some people keep racing pigeons in their backyards. Domestic cats are generally not confined to the house and declawing them is unheard of. Be prepared for looks of confusion when you describe your feline as a "house cat," followed by looks of horror when you explain that its front claws were removed to protect your furniture. British cats come and go as they please (unless they're in a high-rise) by means of a cat flap, usually in the back kitchen door. These flaps produce gales of freezing air in the winter, so people keep the kitchen-to-living-room door closed. Cats are often referred to as "moggies" for some reason.

  A favorite in the pet department, which is not too common in the United States, is the budgerigar, commonly called a "budgie." These tiny birds look like small parakeets and can be hilarious, in that they are often taught to repeat outrageous phrases and usually do so at the most inopportune moments.

BRITISH WORDS THAT MIGHT REQUIRE TRANSLATION

Airing cupboard *n*—linen closet
Bed-sit *n*—studio apartment/efficiency
Bin *n*—trash can (either outside or inside)

Bin bag *n*—trash bag

Bin liner *n*—trash bag

Bin men *n*—trash collectors

Bog *n*—toilet

Bottom drawer *n*—hope chest

Box *n*—TV

Bungalow *n*—ranch-style, single-level houses

Commode *n*—only ever a hospital-type portable toilet

Cot *n*—crib

Cloakroom *n*—can mean a bathroom or a place to hang coats

Council housing—housing project

Cupboard *n*—closet

Des res (pronounced "dez rez") *n*—desirable residence (tongue-in-cheek)

Detached house *n*—single-family house

Dustbin *n*—trash can (outdoor variety)

Dustmen *n*—trash collectors

Duvet *n*—comforter

En suite—refers to a bathroom directly attached to a bedroom

Flat *n*—apartment; condo

French windows *n*—French doors

Garden *n*—yard

Housing estate *n*—housing development (usually newer houses)

Khazi *n*—toilet

Lavatory *n*—toilet

Loft *n*—space at the top of a house that has not been converted into livable space

Loo, lavvy, bog, privy, WC—toilet

Love seat *n*—antique seat with one chair facing one way and the other in the opposite direction (not a simple two-seater as in the States)

Ottoman *n*—blanket chest (usually found in bedrooms)

Outhouse *n*—outside toilet

Parafin *n*—kerosene

Postman *n*—mail carrier

Privet hedge *n*—box wood

Puffy/pouffe *n*—ottoman, foot rest

Rubbish bin *n*—trash can

Scullery *n*—old word for kitchen

Semi-detached house *n*—duplex

Skip *n*—Dumpster

Skirting board *n*—baseboard

Single bed *n*—twin bed

Strimmer *n*—weed whacker

Tap *n*—faucet

Terraced house *n*—row house

Twin beds *n*—two beds in the same room

Wall to wall (carpet) *n*—fitted carpet

Wastepaper basket *n*—trash can (only for paper)

Wheelie bin *n*—outdoor trash can with wheels

Yard *n*—brick, cement-walled enclosure

Zed bed *n*—fold-up bed

AMERICAN WORDS THAT THE BRITS DON'T SHARE

"A" frame house—doesn't exist

Apartment—flat

Baseboard—skirting board

Blanket chest—ottoman

Brownstone/greystone—not used to describe a house like this

Closet (in bedroom)—wardrobe

Closet (anywhere else)—cupboard

Comforter—duvet

Cot—camp bed

Condo—flat

Crib—cot

Dumpster—skip

Faucet—tap

Half-bath—toilet, lavatory, etc.

Hope chest—bottom drawer

Housing project—council estate

Love seat—two-seater sofa

Mud room—utility room

Ranch style—bungalow

Row house—terraced house

Single family dwelling—detached house

Studio apartment—bed-sit

Trash can—bin, rubbish bin, dustbin, wastepaper basket

Twin bed—single bed

Walk-up—not used to describe this type of building, although they do exist

Yard—garden

8

Grub and Other Delicacies

NOW THIS IS where you'll really feel like a foreigner! In the UK, Hush Puppies are a type of comfy shoe and a sloppy joe is a sweater. The Brits won't have a clue about po' boys, grits, or mud pies, but then bubble and squeak, ploughman's lunch, and spotted dick are probably a mystery to you.

In this chapter, I'll walk you through each meal of the day, pointing out the types of strange food you might be served up while in the UK. I'll also let you know which of your favorite American foods you won't find there, and talk about the customs and culture surrounding food in Britain.

- Before we even discuss specific food items, let me tell you that there's sometimes a difference in the *order* in which things are eaten. For example, at a dinner party, the cheese plate will come at the end of the meal, either before, instead of, or after dessert, and will be served with coffee—and port, if you're lucky. Salad is quite often served after the main course.

- Another difference is *how* certain things are eaten. You'll find, in the UK—and other countries in Europe, come to think of it—that people are not too worried about having their salad and the rest of the meal on the same plate. In fact, if you entertain Brits at your home and set out a separate salad plate, you might find that no one has used it when you come to clear the table. It's probably for this reason that there's no salad plate or salad fork in a British place setting.

- Something else to bear in mind about how things are consumed in the UK is the use of both knife and fork. In informal situations it's okay to cut up all your food and then eat with the fork only, although some people might make comments about the similarity to babies having their food cut up for them. However, if you are in a very formal setting, you might want to hold on to both knife and fork and eat like a grown-up.

- Breakfast: Typically, Brits don't eat doughnuts and other sweet sticky stuff first thing in the morning. A "cooked" breakfast will consist of something like fried bacon, sausages, scrambled or fried eggs, fried tomatoes, and baked beans. (By the way, bacon slices are called "rashers.") Kippers, which are smoked herrings, are also a favorite for breakfast in the UK. Toast will be served with a selection of jams and marmalade. The Brits *never* mix sweet and savory breakfast food on the same plate, so watch for their looks of horror when you let your maple syrup drench your sausages! Cereal is the most common daily breakfast, with the heavier, cooked breakfast saved as a weekend treat. Unless you're in an American-style diner, pancakes are rarely found on the breakfast table.

Occasionally, in tonier establishments, you'll come across kedgeree for breakfast. This is a delicious dish of rice, smoked haddock, and egg, which you should certainly sample if you can.

- Lunch: Depending on where you are in the UK (usually the North), this meal could be called "dinner." Except for Sundays, lunch is usually a fairly light affair. A word of warning: If you suggest lunch at 11.30 a.m., you'll be met with astonished faces. Lunchtime is not before noon, and sometimes at 1 p.m.; 11.30 a.m. is definitely still the morning.

Sunday lunch is a larger affair, and many friends or family get together at this time. Typically, this meal will be a "roast" (chicken, beef, lamb, or pork) with all the trimmings—roast potatoes, vegetables, Yorkshire pudding and gravy—followed by dessert or "pudding" and sometimes preceded by a pint at the local pub. Actually, more and more Brits now stay at the pub for their Sunday lunch, as the pubs quite often excel at this fare. (See Pubs at p. 100 in the next chapter.)

Wherever they're from in the UK, all Brits use the term "dinner ladies" to refer to the lovely ladies who serve hot lunches in school cafeterias. (Excessively fat female upper arms are often called "dinner lady arms" or "bingo wings.") For the same unfathomable reason, hot school lunches are referred to as "school dinners" all over the country.

- Dinner: Again, depending on your locale, this meal can be called tea, dinner, or supper. It is usually the heaviest meal of the day. Not as many people eat out in the UK, especially during the week, but if you really can't face cooking every night there is a fabulous selection of ready-to-serve food in most supermarkets—and it's not all diet foods, either. Since adults generally eat out without children, if you are making plans to meet someone for a meal, it's very unusual to schedule dinner before 7 p.m.

- Tea: So what is this tea business, anyway? As I mentioned, in some parts of the country an early evening meal is known as "tea," so if you're invited to tea, it could be a fairly full meal, or just tiny sandwiches, creamy cakes, and posh cups. If you are invited to the posh version, don't panic! Apart from learning how to place a china cup in its saucer without shattering it, there's really nothing to it. Your host will basically wheel out the goodies and the tea, and Bob's your uncle! As with any meal, leave the sweet stuff till last. If you insist on hosting a tea yourself, there are tons of "how-to" books and magazines to help. The main thing to remember is that it's not supposed to be a torture session for you or your guests.

  A "cream tea" refers to the traditional Devonshire tea, which consists of scones served with clotted cream and jam, along with your pot of tea. Clotted cream is thick, yellow cream with the consistency of soft or whipped butter. It is made entirely from the cream of cows' milk and doesn't taste like any cream I've had in the States. Originally this cream used to be made only in Devon but it is now made and sold throughout the country.

  A note about "high tea"—in the UK, this term isn't really used much any more and means anything but posh.

"High tea" actually refers to the heavier version that workers would have when they came in from the fields or the
factory, in the late afternoon. Before bedtime, they would
probably have a top-up of food in the form of "supper."

- Still on the subject of tea—Brits drink more tea than you
can imagine! Most people use tea bags, although some still
prefer loose tea leaves, which require a teapot and strainer.
You will probably be amazed at the quantity of tea consumed in the UK. People pop the kettle on whenever they
have guests, feel under stress, are tired, or just plain bored.
There's always a reason! Most people drink tea with a little
milk, and some just have it black. Few people drink it with
lemon, or anything else, for that matter. If you spend any
length of time in the UK, you'll probably come back a true
convert.

- Because of the ethnic mixes in the UK, the Brits actually
eat a wide variety of foods on a regular basis. Chinese, Italian, and Indian dishes, in particular, are common fare in
homes, but even Japanese and Mexican foods have made a
significant entrance in recent years.

- Cooking: A British recipe book (yes, they exist!) will pose a
few problems for most Americans, not least because they're
now all in metric. There'll be ingredients and instructions
that require interpretation. My advice (seriously) is to have
a UK dictionary handy whenever you tackle a British
recipe. Better still, grab yourself a metric conversion chart
and you'll be a lot safer. Many recipes state the "Gas Mark"
setting so make sure you have found a recipe book that
converts these into centigrade and/or Fahrenheit. The famous *Joy of Cooking* (Simon & Schuster, Inc.) does a great

job of explaining many of the differences between American and British cookery methods and terminology.

Not only will you need to take a conversion chart with you, but also a "cup" measure, as this measurement simply does not exist in the UK. If you ever ask your neighbor for a cup of sugar, there's no telling how much you'll get since it will depend on the size of the cup she uses. (Incidentally, a "cup" in the UK is the word for a piece of apparel—the sports "box"!)

- American food you won't find in Britain: As I've said, po'boys, grits, and Mississippi mud pies could be names of American rock bands as far as most Brits are concerned. Other foods you'll rarely find in Britain are: brittle, sloppy joe, hushpuppies, English muffins, s'mores, Graham crackers, half and half, and anything "over easy." Bisquick now seems to be fairly easy to get hold of, thank goodness! If you're desperate for American fare, there are many Web sites that will deliver stuff to your door.

- There'll be a lot of British food you'll never have encountered before, but I urge you to try everything at least once, as many things look and sound disgusting but are actually quite tasty. These include, but are not limited to— mincemeat pies (actually very sweet fruit pies), picallilli, digestive biscuits, Cornish pasties, Bakewell tarts, Lancashire hotpot, Scotch eggs, Welsh rarebit, Ribena, Lucozade, ginger beer, cockaleekee, black pudding, haggis, bubble and squeak, tripe, ploughman's lunch, and faggots. I won't tell you what they are as that would spoil the element of danger. Why don't you take this list and make it your mission to sample each item during your stay?

- Although many foods can be found in both countries, they often have totally different names, just to confuse visitors (see the glossary below for the more straightforward ones). Alternatively, some foods use the same names but are just pretending to be similar.
    - Pancakes in the UK are more like crepes. In addition, they are typically filled with something sweet and served as dessert. If you're desperate for an American pancake, "drop scones" come fairly close. Now that Bisquick is available, you can also make your own.
    - Chips as Americans know them are "crisps" in the UK, and the variety of flavors you will encounter will either disgust or amaze you—ketchup, savory beef, and sweet and sour are some of the tamer options. The British "chips" are what Americans call French fries. This is worth remembering when you are ordering food.
    - Gravy in the UK is only ever brown, and never served with biscuits. Do try some of the thicker brown gravies, which are served over roast meats—delicious!
    - Talking of biscuits—in the UK they are what you know as cookies. American biscuits look more like British scones, but would never be served on a plate with a meal. British scones are sweet and usually served with jam (jelly) and cream.
    - From time to time you'll find something that *has* the same name but is not the same food item, e.g., coffee cake. In the States this does not seem to require an ounce of coffee in the ingredients, but in the UK it will appear more like a coffee-tasting pound cake or gâteau.

BRITISH WORDS THAT MIGHT
REQUIRE TRANSLATION

Aubergine *n*—eggplant

Banger *n*—sausage

Barbie (BBQ) *n*—grill

Beaker *n*—mug (usually plastic)

Bicarbonate of soda (bicarb) *n*—baking soda

Biscuit *n*—cookie

Blancmange *n* **(pronounced "blamonj")**—thick custard, usually a layer in a trifle

Brew *n*—cup or pot of tea

Broad bean *n*—fava bean

Brown sauce—steak sauce

Bucks Fizz *n*—Mimosa

Butty *n*—sandwich

Candy floss *n*—cotton candy

Castor sugar *n*—very fine sugar

Chipolata *n*—small, pork sausage

Chips *n*—French fries

Chicory *n*—endive

Chip butty *n*—French fry sandwich (truly!)

Cling film *n*—Saran wrap

Coriander *n*—cilantro

Cordial *n*—a thick drink that should be diluted with lots of water (usually for kids and also called juice or "squash")

Cornflour *n*—corn starch

Cos lettuce (pronounced "koss") *n*—the equivalent of iceberg lettuce

Courgette *n* **(pronounced "korjett")**—zucchini

Crisps *n*—chips

Crumpet *n*—resembles an English muffin

Cuppa *n*—cup of tea

Doner kebab *n*—like a Gyro

Double cream *n*—whipping cream

Dressing *n*—can mean either salad dressing or stuffing

Egg timer *n*—hourglass

Fairy cake *n*—cup cake

Fish fingers *n*—fish sticks

Gammon *n*—a large ham

Gherkin (silent "h") *n*—pickle

Ice lolly *n*—Popsicle on a stick

Ice pop *n*—Popsicle

Icing sugar *n*—confectioner's or powered sugar

Jacket potato *n*—baked potato

Jam *n*—jelly

Jelly *n*—Jell-o

Joint *n*—roasted meat (large piece of)

Kebab *n*—kabob

Lemonade *n*—a clear, fizzy drink like 7-up

Madeira cake *n*—pound cake

Mange tout (pronounced *"monj too"*) *n*—snow peas

Marrow *n*—like a huge zuchinni

Minced meat *n*—ground meat

"Neat" *a*—straight (drinks)

Plonk *n*—cheap wine

Pork scratchings *n*—pork rinds

Porridge *n*—oatmeal

Pudding *n*—either dessert course or a heavy pudding

Rapeseed *n*—canola

Rashers *n*—strips of bacon

Rissole *n*—a fried patty containing (usually) leftover food, e.g., fish or meat and potatoes

Rosie Lee *n*—tea (well-known Cockney rhyming slang)

Runner beans *n*—stringy green beans

Sausage roll *n*—sausage wrapped in flaky pastry

Saveloy *n*—long, seasoned sausage

Savoury *a*—the opposite of sweet when describing taste

Scoff *v*—to gobble up

Scone *n*—biscuit; British scones are never served with gravy, only clotted cream and jam

Skate *n*—very common white fish

Soya *n*—soy

Spring onion *n*—green onion

Squash *n*—concentrated fruit juice that must be diluted with water before drinking

Swede *n*—yellow turnip

Swiss roll *n*—jelly roll

UHT milk—long life milk (Ultra Heat Treated) that keeps for several months

Victoria sponge cake *n*—two very light rounded cakes with jam (jelly) between them

"99" *n*—an ice cream with a flaky chocolate stick in the top

AMERICAN WORDS THAT THE BRITS DON'T SHARE

Canola—rapeseed

Confectioner's sugar—icing sugar

Chicory—endive

English muffin—nearest equivalent is a crumpet

Joe (as in "cup of")—coffee

Oleo—margerine

Pound cake—Madeira cake

Produce—green groceries

Skillet—frying pan

Soy—soya

Wiener—Sausage or hot dog

Yellow cake—not unlike the consistency of a Victoria sponge, but be warned—the Brits will fall about when you call it yellow cake

9

Dining (In or Out)

THE GOOD NEWS is that you can find many American chains, if you feel the need for home comforts. The first international TGI Fridays was opened in Birmingham, and they are to be found in most major cities, along with McDonald's, Burger King, Taco Bell, etc. There are also Starbucks popping up all over the place, although the prices may startle you.

Dining out in the United States is usually a much more casual affair than in the United Kingdom. This is probably because it is more expensive in the UK and people treat it more as an evening out than just a means to feed themselves. When booking a table to eat out, it would be unusual to do so for earlier than 7 p.m.

- Although the UK is embracing fast food there are still geographical areas that have few truly fast food places, and very few that stay open 24 hours. It often shocks and amazes Americans that these places will close down or run out of food in the middle of the day when masses of people are clearly waiting to buy something. Stately homes and other such places open to the public are particularly adept at running out of sandwiches about 20 minutes after they open for lunch. If you have blood sugar problems, or just like to eat frequently, don't assume you'll be able to grab something to eat outside of regular mealtimes.

- Unless you're living or working in central London, expect a much slower pace in restaurants. "Table turnover" is not quite the obsession that it is in the States, so you will not be immediately pounced upon to make a menu choice, nor will you feel much pressure to finish your meal and take care of the bill (check). I often find that Americans end up chasing the waiter down, rather than feeling any pressure to leave the establishment.

- Once you are seated in a restaurant, it is generally not the done thing to get up and leave, unless you need to go to the hospital! Being a foreigner, you could obviously get away with it, and indeed no one can stop you as long as you are not leaving an unpaid bill. The natives, however, wouldn't dream of doing this and would also be highly embarrassed if any member of their party tried to.

When I was first married and living in Dallas, my husband decided he didn't like the menu at a restaurant we had chosen. Such is my British training that I was horrified at the prospect of leaving after we had been seated and made him tell the waiter that I wasn't feeling well, while I tried to look as pale and wan as possible! A year later, while visiting England, I did a similar thing myself, to my brother and sister-in-law. This time, we had only stepped into the entrance lobby and I decided I didn't care for the food on the menu. They were so embarrassed they pretended not to know me!

- To help you manage your expectations in a British restaurant, here's what you will and won't get. Ice is often not served with drinks in restaurants (nor do people have large quantities in their houses). Water is usually not served with a meal and extra cups of coffee with dinner are not usually free, nor is the bread. Iced tea is rarely on the menu and refills certainly wouldn't be free. Restaurants usually don't split dishes, serve things on the side, or mix and match their menus as much as here. You won't usually be able to order two appetizers instead of an entrée. In short, don't expect as much flexibility as you get Stateside, but asking politely could result in your request being granted.

  At one London international airport which shall remain nameless, I had to buy two full meals and sit down in the restaurant because my kids wanted French fries. I couldn't just order the fries because they were only on the menu accompanied by fish sticks, chicken nuggets, etc. I asked the assistant to leave the other food off the plate, as I knew my kids wouldn't eat it, but she said she had to serve me the full meal so that the cashier would know what I was paying for. Needless to say, I was speechless at the inflexibility, not to mention the waste of food.

- Be prepared for fewer culinary descriptions from your waiter or in the menu. A hilarious incident happened to me when dining out with my mother and sibs. The waitress could only tell us that one of the special appetizers was "soup." When I asked what kind of soup it was, she replied that she didn't know, and then poised herself, pencil at the ready, for our order. Since I quite fancied a bowl of soup, I asked her if she could find out its flavor. She seemed greatly put out, and my family, I perceived, were slightly embarrassed, too. Good thing I bothered, though, as it was French Onion, which none of us liked.

- Although there are great "takeaway" restaurants (Chinese, Indian, and the famed "chippy") in every town, village, and city, most regular restaurants do not offer doggy bags (which incidentally is an unknown term). If you ask for something to be "wrapped," you will be met with blank looks and a distinct lack of action. Even when you explain what you want, you'll probably be told they don't have anything to put the food in. In addition, rather than delivering this answer apologetically, you'll more than likely be regarded as greedy or crazy. Even where "wrapped" food is available, most Brits haven't embraced this practice.

- You will never be expected to keep your silverware from one course to the next. Indeed, placing your dirty knife and fork on the tablecloth as the busboy approaches would be similar to tipping your plate upside down. In addition, your plate will probably not be removed until you have set your knife and fork next to each other on the plate. Resting silverware apart on your plate indicates that you are still eating your meal.

Talking of silverware—first of all, unless you're talking about family heirlooms, it's "cutlery"; second, although it's becoming more acceptable to cut up your food and then eat it all with only the fork, I would still advise against doing this is in posh restaurants or at formal dinners. Just like elbows on the table, it's not considered good form in the UK.

- When ordering tea or coffee, Brits use the phrases "white," "black," and variations thereof:

  White—coffee/tea with milk
  White without—coffee/tea with milk and no sugar
  Black without—black coffee/tea without sugar
  White with—coffee/tea with milk and sugar
  Black with—black coffee/tea with sugar

  Both tea and coffee are served with milk, as opposed to cream or half and half. If you ask for cream, after some odd looks, you will be given a small jug of very thick cream; half and half is not known. The Brits rarely drink tea with lemon and you would have to ask for it specifically. Similarly, iced tea is not popular in the UK and not often offered as a beverage choice.

  If you make someone a cup of tea in your home, play it safe and ask your guest how he or she likes it beforehand. If you're making it "in the cup" (as opposed to a full pot), *never* use more than one tea bag per cup. If your guest likes strong tea, simply leave the tea bag in the water a little longer. Better still, ask them to "say when." If you're having tea with someone who says, "Shall I be Mother?" (even if it's a guy), they are simply offering to pour the tea!

  A final point on tea: You'll discover there are many different opinions about how the perfect cup of tea is made, but one thing is for certain—microwaved water just doesn't cut it with most Brits. If you don't possess a kettle, it's better to boil the water in a small saucepan than to risk the microwave.

- When buying a sandwich, you will typically not be presented with the number of options that you get in the States. Perhaps you'll be asked if you'd like white or brown bread, but the salad (lettuce and tomato) will be included unless you can catch them beforehand. If you have particular likes or dislikes, be very upfront and specific about them, or you'll just have to take what you get—the Brits are not as relaxed about making you up another sandwich just because you don't like it. Many Americans find the skinny British sandwiches highly amusing. I must enlighten you here, though—those pathetic, skinny sandwiches are usually only sold in business areas where starving office workers have little or no choice but to put up with them. Take yourself off to a real bakery or tea shop and you'll find some huge, bun-style "sarnies" with delicious fillings spilling out all over the place.

- Brits very rarely have breakfast outside of their home, except in London, where brunch has caught on. Unless you're in an American-type restaurant, don't expect to be understood if you ask for eggs "sunny side up" or any other similar description. Eggs come basically fried, scrambled, poached, or boiled: after that, you need to describe how you'd like them cooked in plain, old-fashioned English.

- When you've finished your meal, ask for the "bill" rather than the "check," as some wait staff might think you're referring to a method of payment, which incidentally you are allowed to use in restaurants backed up by a bank card— and the spelling is "cheque."

- In many restaurants in the UK you must order every part of your meal individually. Often, the meat entrée doesn't "come with" veggies or potatoes and you'll have to remember to order them. In pubs and gastropubs, however, it is more common to have buffets, or to find a full meal on the menu. It is legal for minors aged sixteen and seventeen to be bought a beer or cider to drink with a meal. This applies to restaurants but not bars.

- Tipping: Check your restaurant or hotel bill to see if a service charge has already been added, in which case there is no need to tip further, and certainly not the rigid 15 percent as here. If you feel the service has been unacceptable, you may refuse to pay the service charge, and you will rarely be interrogated or followed outside if the tip appears small. You will, however, see an extra charge for VAT (explained below) on your bill.

- When referring to food or a restaurant, the phrase "cordon bleu" is pronounced in the French style and the Brits will be highly amused to hear "cordon bloo."

BEING ENTERTAINED AT SOMEONE'S HOUSE

- You may be invited to a "dinner party" even though only four to six people are invited. This is considered a fairly formal invitation, which requires a timely response, prompt arrival, and no unannounced extra guests. Unless otherwise stated, it will usually be an adults-only invitation, so don't drag your kids along even if you can't find a baby-sitter. It is customary to take a bottle of wine or a small gift, or as one American friend puts it, it is "the kiss of death" to arrive empty-handed. It is also good manners to call or write afterwards to say thank you.

- Your hostess may say "Seven-thirty for eight," or, "Eight for eight-thirty," which means that you can turn up any time *within* this half hour. You should not wander in late. A very formal invitation may state, "Mrs. John Doe at home for Jane," which basically means the parents are throwing a posh party for lucky old Jane. At a dinner party, expect to have the seating allocated by the host; a common practice is for couples to be split up.

- If invited to "supper," this will be around the same time but will be a much more casual affair. "Casual" does *not* mean you can turn up late, though.

- Whatever type of invitation you receive, while it is courteous to offer to bring something, it is not common to bring a complete course, such as a salad or dessert. *Do not* insist if your host says not to worry. Insisting that you contribute to the meal is just not done in the UK, unless it's family or really close friends; even then, you'll often find the hosts want to do it themselves. Similarly, by all means help clear the table, but remember you are there to socialize, so spending the rest of the night in the kitchen clearing up will make your hosts feel uncomfortable, force them to join you in clearing up, and ruin what might have been a relaxing evening.

- If you receive an invitation to a dinner party that you can't make, don't be surprised or offended if the host simply says, "Oh, never mind, another time perhaps." Unless the host is specifically trying to introduce you to certain people, the dinner party will go on without you.

- Evening socializing usually goes on later than it does in the United States and dinner parties often don't start till 8.30 p.m. nor break up till after midnight. Formal balls typically go on into the wee hours of the morning and a breakfast will be served. When an American friend threw her first dinner and invited guests for 7 p.m., one English guest commented that it was an "odd" time to serve dinner.

- Unless you are entertaining business clients, taking friends out to dinner and paying for their meals is not considered "entertaining one's friends" and is rarely done.

- The table settings in the UK are a little different from their American equivalents. For a start, there will be no salad plate or fork, and no long-handled spoon set at the side next to the knife. (Southerners—What *is* that for anyway?) All knives will be to the right and all forks (except a dessert fork) to the left. If you're having soup, you will also get a soup spoon next to your knife. Across the top will be the dessert spoon and possibly a fork. If in doubt, just surreptitiously copy the majority at the table. When you have a multitude of knives and forks set out before you, the secret is to work from the outside in. The great thing about being an American dining in the UK is that you can cover yourself ahead of time by explaining that the table settings are different, and would somebody please advise you.

- The order of food in the UK may be slightly different from what you're used to in the States. For example, you'd rarely be offered a plate of cheese to nibble on before the meal, as cheese is usually served at the end, sometimes with a glass of port. Be advised—if you have never had port before, it is a fortified wine and packs a strong punch the morning after. When the port does appear at the table, it should be passed around to the left. If you decided not to imbibe, you should still pass the decanter around rather than placing it in the center of the table. In the olden days, when the port came out, it was time for the ladies to retire to another room and let the men do their thing. This rarely happens these days.

- The question, "Would you like a drink?", can lead to some confusion and embarrassment. Many hosts will be referring to an alcoholic drink, especially in the evening, but during the day it could well be a cup of tea. Best way around this one? Reply with something like "Whatever's easiest," and take your cue from them. If you're doing the hosting and your polite guest asks for tea when you had something stronger in mind, give him another chance by adding, "Would you prefer something stronger?" You should be warned that the coffee you'll be served might well be instant, as Brits drink a lot of instant coffee. If it's real, it will more likely be made in a cafetiere than a drip coffee maker. Fortunately, it tastes the same.

- Potluck dinners do occur, but they are not called potluck. I have heard them called "bottle and plate" parties, and there are sure to be more variations on that theme. Similarly, a "brown bag" lunch exists but is usually called simply a "packed lunch," and no one uses the term "family style" to describe the way a meal is served.

- If you're invited to a barbecue, be prepared to be disappointed. For obvious reasons (the weather), BBQs aren't as common as they are in the States, therefore people aren't as proficient. The fare is usually limited to charred sausages, chicken, and hamburgers. If you take fancier food along to be grilled, I would advise taking care of it yourself. "Cookout" is not a recognized term in the UK.

PUBS

Although not always thought of as a place to dine, it's time to turn our attention to the good old pub. In the UK, the pub is the center of local activity and communication. You'll find one just about anywhere you go—indeed, some of them seem so remote, you'll wonder where the customers (called "regulars") come from. Invariably, when you arrange to meet someone socially, it'll be in a pub (although Starbucks and the like are becoming more common).

These days, more and more pubs are serving food. Some have a restaurant section and you won't be able to order food to eat at the bar. Others serve food in all areas of the bar, and the rising complaint is that it's getting difficult just to go for a drink these days. Despite the woeful reputation of British cuisine in general, pub food is often surprisingly good. Although I generalize here, pub food is usually hot, hearty, and good value, if not the healthiest of victuals.

The latest phenomenon in the UK gastronomic world is the evolution of the gastropub. These pubs originated in London about twenty years ago, when pub owners were desperately trying to think of ways to pull in money. There are still many more gastropubs in London than anywhere else, but there are plenty dotted all over the country and Web sites galore to help you find them. Many of these gastropubs are very old or picturesque pubs with great chefs on board. Definitely worth scouting one out.

- First things first—if you're only there for a drink, always go to the bar when trying to order. Bars in the UK don't have wandering waitresses, although some will let you run up a tab, or "put it on the bill." A warning here: While the bar may be the only place where the Brits don't seem to be "queuing," customers will definitely know who got there first, second, and so on. If you try to jump this invisible queue, the barman will probably ignore you and serve the person who is *really* next. To ensure getting served, simply rest your elbow on the bar (if you can get near it) and hold out your empty glass or money. This must be done very casually, though. The barman (or woman) will let you know when you are about to be served by looking at you as he's serving the current customer. You should then indicate that you've seen this with a slight nod of the head, a smile, or any other subtle gesture. Pushing and shoving is allowed, if it's a really busy bar. It also helps to be about six inches taller than the people in front of you.

- While drinking in a bar (or pub) you are not expected to leave a tip on the bar; indeed, you will receive some very strange looks if you do. Sometimes patrons offer to buy the bar staff a drink ("And one for yourself") but this is not expected. If you do, the bar staffer (who may not be permitted to drink while on duty) will thank you, tell you what they like, and charge you accordingly. As of November 24, 2005, pubs, bars, clubs, and shops may apply for a license to serve alcohol twenty-four hours per day.

- If you plan to frequent pubs, you might want to acquaint yourself with the stuff on offer. Asking for a beer is more likely to result in a dark brown, slightly warm liquid also known as "bitter." Lighter, American-style beers are known as "lager," and are often much stronger than you're used to, so be warned. You'll also be expected to state your quantity when ordering beer, e.g., half a pint or a pint. Despite the rumored advances in women's lib, most women over thirty-five don't drink pints!

- Most pub staff won't know how to serve elaborate cocktails (unless you include gin and tonic or vodka and orange), although if you can give them ingredients and quantities, they'll usually be more than happy to give yours a try. Wine bar staff are more likely to have a repertoire of cocktails up their sleeves.

- Warning: Cider is never non-alcoholic. It refers to an exceedingly potent apple derivative, and if from the West Country ("Scrumpy"), it is even more lethal.

- Fifteen minutes before closing time, the bar manager will shout something like "Last orders, please," which means that if you want another drink, you'd better be quick. After fifteen minutes he or she will shout, "Time, please," or, "Time, ladies and gentlemen, please," to let you know that you must finish your drinks and leave. By law, pubs are supposed to be empty fifteen minutes after this, so many bar managers will appear very aggressive in trying to get you to leave. In central London, where the pubs tend to be packed to the gills, there are a handful that set off their fire alarms—the noise is so loud that you'll even leave a full pint to get away from it! The bouncers at many pubs not only vet who comes in but make sure everyone leaves when they're supposed to.

- Now that pubs can serve alcohol all night, the time-honored and illicit practize of the "lock-in" is redundant. The owner or manager used to invite patrons to stay after closing hours, and pretend not to *sell* drinks but to offer them as to a friend. There are various Web sites and blogs bemoaning the demise of the lock-in.

BRITISH WORDS THAT MIGHT REQUIRE TRANSLATION

Afters *n*—dessert

Ball *n*—a very formal (black tie) affair

BBQ'd *a*—grilled

Bevvy *n*—alcoholic drink (beverage)

Boozer *n*—the pub; can also describe someone who drinks a lot

Chippy *n*—fish and chip shop

Claret *n*—red Bordeaux wine

Cutlery *n*—silverware

Fillet *n*—same meaning, but Brits pronounce the "t"

Grilled *a*—broiled (not BBQ'd)

Hock *n*—German white wine

Main course *n*—entrée

"My shout" *n*—"My round"

Off license (offie) *n*—liquor store

PBAB (Please bring a bottle)—BYOB

Packed lunch *n*—brown bag or sack lunch

Plonk *n*—cheap wine

Pudding *n*—dessert course or a heavy pudding

RSVP (Répondez, s'il vous plait)—Please reply

Scrumpy *n*—wickedly strong West Country cider

Serviette *n*—napkin (napkin is also used)

Speciality (note extra syllable) *n*—specialty

Starter *n* appetizer
Sweet (course) *n*—dessert course
Take-away *n*—"to go"
Tomato sauce *n*—ketchup

AMERICAN WORDS THAT THE BRITS DON'T SHARE

Appetizer—starter
Broiled—grilled
Brown bag—packed lunch
Busboy and bussing—totally meaningless in the UK
Catsup—ketchup
Cookout—BBQ
Doggy bag—doesn't exist
Entrée—main course
Grilled—BBQ'd
Half and half—cream
Ketchup—tomato sauce
Liquor store—off license
Potluck—bottle + plate party
Tailgate—nobody does this
"To go"—take-away
Silverware—cutlery
Wet bar—bar
86 it—not used

RESOURCES

There are many, many online restaurants and pub information services. Simply by typing in a few search words, you'll be hit with more sites than you really want. Here are a few that I like:

www.gastropubs.tablesir.com—Site containing a handful of great gastropubs
www.restaurantguides.co.uk—Site providing free services such as venue scouting and booking, restaurant and bar reviews
www.bbc.co.uk/food—The BBC's food Web-site, which contains information on restaurant openings around the country, as well as telling you what foods are in season and what's healthy for your kids to eat

And don't forget the *Good Food Guide, Egon Ronay's Guide,* and the *Michelin Hotel and Restaurant Guide*—probably the three highest-profile reviewers of restaurants in the UK

10

That's Entertainment

You'll probably find that people in the UK are less engaged in the pursuit of entertainment than the average American. You'll rarely hear them asking each other, "What are your plans for the weekend?" Sundays are typically very laid-back, family affairs, with the occasional pint at the local pub before going home for Sunday lunch or dinner. Having said that, Brits do have a great many ways of entertaining themselves; and as usual, there are a great many unwritten rules you'll need to know.

- First things first: The term "theatre" always refers to a stage production, and not the movies. (Also note the spelling!) You might get a few invitations to go to "the pictures," which means a movie theatre or cinema. An older word, but one that is still used for the movies, is "the flicks."
- The theatre in the UK is first class. Obviously, there's London's West End and Shakespeare's Stratford-upon-Avon,

but don't write off provincial theatre. "The provinces" have great shows, particularly if a play is touring before going on to a London theater. The Royal Shakespeare Company considers Newcastle-upon-Tyne one of its major venues after Stratford and London. Unlike the States, the cast usually doesn't change when the production moves to a new city, so you have a chance of seeing the "stars" even outside London.

Theater shows usually begin on time; if late, you must often wait until the interval (intermission) to take your seat. Tickets for the big London shows are often hard to come by, but the theatres do sell off cut-price tickets for that night's performance, so it is possible to get lucky. Oh yes, when you see a sign for the "Stalls" in the theatre, it's referring to the orchestra, or ground-level seats. The "Circle" or "Royal Circle" refers to the mezzanine; "Upper Circle" means the Balcony; the "Gallery" is the Upper Balcony; and "the Gods" are the nosebleed seats.

- One particular piece of theatre you may not be familiar with is the good old "pantomime" or "panto." This is not actually a mime at all, though you will find it most peculiar. Typically performed around Christmastime, it is a lavish performance of a well-known fairy story, such as *Cinderella, Mother Goose, Snow White,* etc. Many famous British personalities star in these pantomimes and take them on tour around the country. Think of them as precursors to the modern musicals such as *Cats* and *Phantom.*

There are a few oddities about these pantomimes that you should know of. First, and perhaps most odd, the male lead (called the principal boy), such as Prince Charming in *Cinderella,* is often played by a female. Every now and then you'll get a female impersonator *pretending* to be a female in the principal boy role! If there are any old hags to be played, such a witches and wicked stepmothers, you can guarantee they'll be played by men. The second odd thing is the banter. Throughout the pantomime, not only will there be many references to current affairs (which could make you feel like a stranger within the first five minutes), but the players will invariably turn to the audience and yell something like, "Oh no, you wouldn't," to which the audience will join in with, "Oh yes, I would!" Fortunately, the many risqué jokes included go over the heads of the little ones and pantos are generally good, safe family entertainment.

- For those of you who haven't visited the UK in a while, British TV has come a long way. For a start, there are now numerous "terrestrial" channels (not satellite or cable), and almost round-the-clock coverage. In addition, most homes now have either satellite or cable channels, allowing you access to many of your favorite American TV shows, as well as a wide variety of European soccer matches. Better than all the TV shows are the commercials (adverts), which people watch as avidly as any soap. They are often much more risqué than anything you'd see in the States, and the humor is exceedingly dry.

    If you have occasion to buy or lease a TV, make sure you also purchase a TV license. Since the BBC channels don't run commercials, they generate revenue via the dreaded license. Yes, it is possible to operate a TV without a license, but if you're caught in the act, you'll receive a hefty fine. (TV detector vans roam the streets and can pick up the signal from your home.) You only need one license per house, no matter how many TVs you have in there, and licenses can be purchased at Post Offices, by phone, mail or online. (By the way, the noun "license" is spelled "licence" in the UK; the verb is still "license.") Under recent licensing regulations, people using PCs to watch television are still required to obtain a television license.

- The National Lottery: It will appear to you that the Brits are obsessed with their National Lottery. There are several lotteries—daily, weekly, bi-monthly, and monthly—all with different names for players' ease. You can play online (if you're over sixteen), and buy lottery tickets everywhere. When the winning numbers are picked, it is done with much fanfare as a nationally televised half hour show. The winners get 50 percent of the monies paid into the lottery, while about 28 percent of this pool helps fund projects and grants throughout the UK.

- Turf accountants—otherwise known as betting shops or "bookies," can be found throughout the land as the British love to place bets. Aside from the usual things to bet on, such as horse racing and soccer results, you can currently place bets on who will be the next pope or the next American president. The term "punter" is very common in the UK; it used to refer specifically to gamblers but is now used for customers in general.

- The local pub is often the center of entertainment for many people. The bars in the States that claim to be authentic English or Scottish pubs are actually nothing like those in the UK. For a start, British pubs are usually carpeted. If the pub is a tad grotty, your feet will stick to the carpet as you make your way to the bar. If it's a really old country pub, you might see the original flagstone floor.

The pub is a good place to meet friends and sit and have a chat. Many, particularly in small towns and villages, have their own darts competitions, football teams, quiz nights, and snooker and cricket teams, which play in pub leagues. (I kid you not!)

Of course, there's the other type of pub—noisy, bright, and full of young people out on the town for the night. Most major towns and cities have fairly active social scenes, again with the pub at the center of it all. You'll also find quite a few wine bars, where you can get snacks or even a meal with your glass of vino, and, if you're lucky, you'll be able to hear enough to have a conversation.

- The laws governing alcohol consumption are very different in the UK. It is illegal to give alcohol to a child under five unless it's an emergency, and there must be adult supervision. Children under fourteen are allowed into bars that have a children's certificate; they must stay in a room or area (e.g., garden) where alcohol is consumed but not sold. In other words they can't belly up to the bar. Always check with the restaurant or pub manager as some establishments still refuse to have children on the premises.

   At ages fourteen and fifteen, minors can go into bars but may not consume alcohol. At sixteen and seventeen they may be bought a beer or cider to eat with a meal but only in restaurants, not pubs. Again, check with the manager beforehand. Eighteen is the legal age at which you may purchase and consume alcohol.

- The UK is sports-mad—unfortunately, not the same sports

that you follow in the United States. Soccer (commonly referred to as "football" in Europe, South America, and basically everywhere but the States) is big, and every city has at least one team. Many have two and the rivalry between them is fierce. Unfortunately, a football match/game is not the place for young kids and grannies. The fans often get quite violent and the atmosphere just isn't the same as at American baseball or football games. Alcohol is not served, nor will you be allowed into a match if you appear inebriated.

Note: a "pitch" in the UK refers to the field where the game is being played, and a "strip" or "kit" is the uniform. The other big team sports in the UK are rugby, cricket, snooker, and darts, which receive a lot of TV coverage and are followed almost as avidly. Track and field sports are covered extensively and participated in at school.

• Apparently the biggest participant sport (as opposed to spectator sport) is fishing—or "angling," as it's also known. For obvious reasons, this is not covered widely on TV, but you *will* see plenty of sheep-dog trials. There used to be a TV show—which was extremely popular and went on for years—called *One Man and His Dog*. The commentator had to speak in an extremely quiet voice so as not to distract the dogs. I'm not joking! Another sport widely participated in, particularly if you're over eighty, is lawn bowling. In every town, city, and village you'll find a beautifully manicured bowling green with little old men and women quietly bowling big black balls toward a smaller white one. People get very serious about their bowling and spend hours out there.

- A few differences in sporting terms: "Hockey" in the UK is generally understood to refer to field hockey. If you want to talk about ice hockey, say "ice hockey." Similarly, "riding" is the term used for horse-back riding, and skiing refers to snow-skiing rather than water-skiing.
- If you're a big knitter you'll be thrilled at the amount of "wool shops" to be found in the UK. Be aware that knitting needle sizes are different in the UK so a British knitting pattern is a potential disaster area. Grab a needle size converter before attempting a British pattern and you won't have to buy a new supply of knitting needles. Yarn is generally called "wool." Similarly, if you're into sewing, remember that British sizing is different so double-check any patterns you buy. Many department stores have fabric and wool departments.
- One thing that will have you rubbing your eyes in disbelief is Morris dancing. This is a centuries old type of folk-dancing done by enthusiasts up and down the country, and indeed in North America and the Antipodes. Its origins are heavily debated and linked to the far corners of the globe; however there are references to Morris dancing in Shakespeare. It is probably the closest to traditional English dancing that there is, although there are huge regional differences both in the dance steps and the costumes. For costumes they are! Probably the closest thing to an English national costume actually. In most cases the men (and a few women) wear knee breaches, baggy shirts and vests. The shirts are almost always white but the breaches can be black or white and the vests can be any color. Some Morris dancers have bells attached to the bottom of their breaches, some wear clogs and some paint their faces black. The

dancers sort of gaily jump around clashing sticks, swords or waving handkerchiefs, accompanied by a variety of instruments closely related to the accordion. Morris dancing is largely associated with May Day celebrations. Teams compete in national and international competitions and are passionate about their hobby. If you look up Morris dancing on the Internet you will see what I mean.

- Another national hobby that you'll find quaint and amusing is the brass band. The celebrated composer, conductor, and wit Sir Thomas Beecham is alleged to have said "Brass bands are all very well in their place—outdoors and several miles away". The British movie "Brassed Off" accurately portrays brass bands in the UK. Generally regarded as a working class hobby, there are competitions around the country to proclaim the best brass band. Many brass bands are affiliated to work situations such as factories and mines, and the band members must be employees to be eligible to compete. Many outdoor parks still have Victorian band stands, and the practice of a brass band playing on Sunday afternoons is being revived in some areas.

- The world of entertainment in general will be very different in the UK. American celebrities who can barely walk along the street in the States without being mobbed are unknown in the UK—apart from the Tom Cruise–type international superstars. Katie Couric, Barbara Walters, Dave Letterman, Sammy Sosa? They would probably only be recognized by fellow Americans. Similarly, the personalities that are featured every week in British gossip columns will ring no bells with you. Don't worry, you'll soon know exactly who Lulu, Denise Van Outen, and Cliff Richards are.

BRITISH WORDS THAT MIGHT
REQUIRE TRANSLATION

Adverts *n*—commercials
(The) baths *n*—swimming pool; swimming baths
"The Beeb"—affectionate name for the BBC
BBC—British Broadcasting Corporation
Booking office *n*—ticket office
Bookmaker/bookies—betting shop
Chat show—talk show
Dobber *n*—remote control
"The flicks" *n*—the movies
Gods *n*—nosebleed seats in the theatre
ITN—Independent Television Network
Kit *n*—sports uniform
Match *n*—game (football, cricket, etc.)
"The pictures" *n*—the movies
Pitch *n*—playing field
Snug *n*—small section in very old bars
Stands *n*—bleachers
Stalls *n*—orchestra seats in the theatre
Strip *n*—sports uniform
Terraces *n*—bleachers (in soccer)

AMERICAN WORDS THAT THE BRITS
DON'T SHARE:

Bleachers—stands
Movie theater—cinema; the pictures
Orchestra seats—Stalls

Pinch hitter—doesn't exist

Ticket office—booking office

Uniform—this word is only used for military, police, and other such professional attire; not sports attire

RESOURCES

www.national-lottery.co.uk—The National Lottery Web site

www.tvlicensing.co.uk—TV licensing is the BBC's agent for television license collection. License fees can be paid online via this Web site

www.direct.gov.uk—Official government Web site giving information about alcohol consumption laws and much more

11

Shop Till You Drop

STORES ARE CALLED "SHOPS"—whether they're quaint candy stores or giant supermarkets. Shopping is about the only thing the Brits do as big as Americans, and most major cities now boast a "hypermarket" (an enormous store selling everything) or huge shopping center within a few miles. Retailers are very into merchandising; therefore, the stores are usually a pleasure to walk around. I've come to expect beautifully stacked shelves and artistic window displays from British shops, especially during the holiday season. At Christmas, every major city boasts a department store window display that could rival a Broadway production. Be sure to take the kids to visit the nearest one to you if you have a chance.

Again, although it may look the same, shopping in the UK has its own set of do's and don'ts, some of which you should definitely know ahead of time.

- Forms of payment: Checks (cheques) are accepted almost everywhere, including restaurants, but must be accompanied by your bank's Cheque Guarantee Card. This guarantees payment of up to £50 by your bank. (When obtaining a checkbook from your UK bank, you should also receive this card.) Your driving license will neither be required nor sufficient to support the check. Needless to say, U.S. checks will not be accepted.

  Credit cards and debit cards are checked much more thoroughly than is usual in the United States, as are matching signatures on cards and checks. Don't be offended if a sales assistant takes time to check all the details—they do it with everyone. You will never be able to use another person's credit card, under any circumstances. While working in the retail industry in London, I often witnessed young Americans on their travels armed with Daddy's credit card and a letter stating they were allowed to use it. Obviously, it never worked, and even when we had a customer service person explain the procedure, the would-be customers were always outraged. Scottish notes are legal tender throughout the UK and must be accepted as payment.

- You may find the return policies in some stores more stringent/less reasonable than in the United States. British people are not used to making a fuss, and shop assistants are not used to people demanding refunds. If you have a bona fide claim, hold your ground and don't let them walk all over you! Always keep your receipts.

  If you really think you have a claim that is being denied by a store, find your local Citizens Advice Bureau or CAB (there is usually one in every city). They will advise you as to your consumer rights, as well as how to go about claiming them. I have had great success myself using this method.

- One of the great things about shopping in the UK is the fact that the price tag you see is the price you pay. (The bad news is that there's a 17.5% VAT tax everywhere.) All taxes are included in the displayed price. No more scrabbling for high school math to work out the price after sales tax. It is not customary to barter for a discount off a given price— but it may not hurt to try.

- Shop assistants do not approach and follow you around the way they do in the States. This is part poorer customer service and part culture—British people don't like a hard sell.

- In most large grocery stores (supermarkets) you may still be required to pack your own groceries at the checkout. More and more large supermarkets have packers; but if there isn't one when your goods are checked out, don't stand around waiting for someone to appear or you'll still be there at closing time. Some stores even charge you for their bags, although this is less and less common.

- Opening and consuming anything before you've paid for it is sometimes considered theft. Security in many stores is quite high and plain-clothed security personnel often follow you around, trying to be inconspicuous!

- The Retail Export Scheme: If you are not a resident (and therefore not required to pay taxes), you are sometimes entitled to reclaim the 17.5% VAT (Value Added Tax) that you pay with every purchase. At the time of purchase, ask the vendor for the relevant form (VAT 407). Since this is a voluntary program, not all vendors participate, so if you really want the tax refund, check with the vendor *before* you make a purchase. Also make sure you have your passport with you, as many vendors will ask for proof of non-residence in the UK. The vendor must complete a portion of this form, and you must then present this form with your receipts to HM (Her Majesty's) Customs and Excise upon leaving the country. Your reimbursement will be forwarded to you. Without this form and your receipts, you will not be able to claim. Leave plenty of time at the airport or port of departure, as there are often queues (lines). Remember not to pack and check the items you are claiming, as the goods must be available for inspection. You must also make this claim within three months of the relevant purchase.

Sometimes you can obtain a cash refund for the tax paid while at your airport of departure, but check beforehand as only a handful of airports do this. A few stores and commercial companies will handle a refund claim for you, and if you're planning to buy a lot of stuff to bring back to the States, it's probably worth at least finding out what they can do for you. Travelex and Equivat are two such companies, although the UK government Web site does a pretty good job of explaining things. (See Resources below for sites.)

- While you may not be able to buy some of your favorite American items, you can usually buy a decent equivalent. If you are planning to be in the UK for more than a few months, I would advise switching to UK brands—it's far cheaper than having stuff mailed. In addition, when having things mailed from the United States, you run the risk of having to pay additional (and hefty) customs charges when they arrive in the UK. Admittedly, there are a few things that will be harder to find, such as large bags of ice, and coolers; but then, you'll rarely need them! Recently,

Internet-based companies have sprung up supplying American goods to the desperate all over the planet. Worth a search.

- Many established American brand names are simply not known in the UK, so any jokes or other references to them will fall flat. While many candy items are sold across the pond, items such as Tylenol, Advil, Clorox (etc.) are not known. Likewise, many British things are known simply by their brand names; indeed, the verb "to vacuum clean" is usually substituted with "to hoover" the carpet.

- Many chains of stores are nationwide (e.g., Asda, Marks & Spencer, BHS, Tesco, Sainsburys, Boots, Safeway). The retail business is extremely competitive. As a result, the stores' own brand merchandise is excellent. Do not be afraid to try their own label food, clothes, pharmaceutical items, and wine. You'll be pleasantly surprised.

- Some excellent bargains can be found in the sales. Retail laws in the UK strictly govern what can be labeled as a sale item. Stores are not allowed to ship in truckloads of inferior merchandise and then pass it off as "reduced to clear" goods. Usually, merchandise has to have been in the store for a significant period of time marked at a higher price before it can be called a sale item.

- There are very few 24-hour stores in the UK. In smaller towns and villages, shops close at 5 p.m. promptly, and some still close for a half day on Wednesdays. Banks and Post Offices are not generally open outside of office hours.

- Most things in the UK are purchased in metric quantities, so you need to translate those imperial recipes before you go out to buy your ingredients. Although most people can still relate to imperial measurements (at least adults can), food containers no longer show the imperial equivalent as a helpful guide.

- If you ever need a duplicate key made, for some reason you'll find that most shoe menders (cobblers) can do this. A few DIY (Home Improvement/Do-It Yourself) stores also have this service, but your best bet is the local cobbler.

- A great tradition on a Sunday morning is the local car boot sale. Usually held in a field or church/rugby club parking lot, people literally load up their car trunks (boots) with the junk they no longer want, and sell it at the boot sale. Nowadays it's becoming a little more up market and the wares are set out on folding tables. Yard sales as seen in the United States do not really exist, although schools and churches often have similar "jumble sales" to raise funds.

BRITISH WORDS THAT MIGHT
REQUIRE TRANSLATION

Cashpoint *n*—ATM

BOGOF—Buy One Get One Free

Cheque *n*—check

Chippie *n*—fish and chip shop or sometimes just the "chip" shop

Chemist *n*—drugstore/pharmacy

Chemist (the person) *n*—pharmacist

Cobbler *n*—shoe mender

DIY (Do-it-yourself) shop *n*—Home Improvement Store

Fish shop *n*—Often refers to the fish and chip shop, but can also mean just a fresh fish shop

Greengrocer *n*—sells only fruit and vegetables

Hole in the wall *n*—ATM (seriously!)

Hypermarket *n*—extremely large store selling just about everything

Jumble sale *n*—garage sale

Newsagent *n*—sells only newspapers, candy, magazines, and some stationery items

Off license ("offie") *n*—liquor store (pubs used to sell liquor to be consumed off the premises)

Punter *n*—used to mean "gambler" but now refers to any customer

Queue *n*—line

Second-hand shop *n*—resale store; thrift shop

Shop *n*—store

Trolley *n*—cart

VAT *n*—Value Added Tax (sales tax)

Wet fish shop *n*—sells fresh fish

AMERICAN WORDS THAT THE BRITS DON'T SHARE

ATM—cashpoint

Cart—trolley

Check—cheque

Drugstore—chemist

Garage sale—jumble sale

Home Improvement store—DIY (Do-it-yourself) store

Line—queue

Pharmacist—chemist

Pharmacy—chemist

Resale store—second-hand shop
Sack—a large Hessian-type bag with a drawstring; never a regular bag

SOME BRAND NAMES WELL KNOWN TO BRITS

Calpol—children's pain reliever/fever reducer
Cling film—Saran wrap
Codeine—painkiller (sold over the counter)
Dettol—antiseptic/disinfectant liquid
Domestos—Clorox-type bleach
Marigolds—rubber gloves, for washing dishes, etc.
Nescafé—instant coffee
Paracetamol—painkiller
TCP—antiseptic liquid
Zimmer frame—walker

RESOURCES

www.consumerdirect.gov.uk—Consumer Direct, run by the Department of Trade and Industry (DTI). Gives consumer information covering everything from cars and food, through travel and finance
www.csnconnect.org.uk—Consumer Support Networks; a collaboration of many advice bodies to help obtain consistent standards across the country. This site provides links to the DTI's Consumer Direct

www.citizensadvice.org.uk—Citizens Advice Bureau (CAB). The CAB gives free advice on a huge range of subjects. The Web site contains a wealth of online information

www.which.net/campaigns/contents.html—Consumers' Association, which campaigns on many issues and gives related information on this site

www.travelex.co.uk—Travelex Web site, acts as an agent for a number of VAT-refunding agents. Found at many airports

www.equivat.com—Equivat Ltd. Web site; another company that can help with VAT refunds

www.visitbritain.com—British Tourist Authority's Web site, with information on claiming VAT refunds and customs procedures

www.rip-off.co.uk—Consumers' Champion Web site, protecting consumers against rip-off pricing

12

At Your Service

TRUTH BE TOLD, the UK is definitely not as service-oriented as the United States, and that's probably one of the first things you'll miss. Except for London, where you can get or do anything 24/7, most cities and towns close down for the night and keep very strict hours. As a customer, you'll rarely be bowled over by a "greeter" either in a store or restaurant, except for the American chains like TGI's and Disney Stores, where you'll find embarrassed Brits trying to act like their American counterparts. Greeters are also popping up in some of the larger supermarkets. The service you'll receive will be a softer sell and definitely slower. Part of this is culture—Brits don't like to be harassed by overeager sales assistants while shopping; and part is that the concept of "customer service" is still dawning on the Brits.

In this chapter, I'll guide you through some of the quainter elements of British service, and help you decide such things as what type of "char" you might need, and if indeed you'll need one at all. I'll explain when the postman comes, and exactly what he can do for you, as well as outlining the (in)famous medical services you'll find in the UK, and the funny names the doctors go by.

- The Royal Mail—Now here's one service you'll definitely appreciate. Although the mail carriers (postmen) won't pick up outgoing mail from your home even if you beg, they will deliver your mail first thing in the morning. Furthermore, any first-class item you mail (post) by 5 p.m. one day will reach its destination (within the UK) the following morning.

  Most houses have a rectangular letterbox (hole in the front door) rather than a mailbox outside or at the end of the yard. If you have a dog that chews everything, or children that get into your stuff, you can purchase a basket which fits on the back of the door and catches the mail before it lands on the floor.

- Mail boxes—The mail boxes (letterboxes) in the UK look entirely different from the smaller blue ones in the States. British letterboxes are huge! They can be found in the middle of the sidewalk (pavement) all over the country; they are about five feet tall, bright red and cylindrical. You really can't miss them. On the front, underneath the opening for your mail, will be the times of daily deliveries. Also be on the lookout for letterboxes in walls. Very often you'll see what looks like a red plaque on the wall, with a rectangular hole in it. This is in fact a compact letterbox, which operates exactly the same as the larger version.

- Post Offices—British Post Offices have a red sign with a

gold crown outside which makes them very easy to spot once you know what you're looking for. Large Post Offices often also sell books, magazines, and stationery items. In smaller towns and villages, your local sub-Post Office will very likely be situated inside another store—this is when you'll need to look for the gold crown sign in the window. Once inside, you'll find a separate line (queue) for the Post Office counter. Don't expect to be able to buy stamps along with your morning newspaper—you need to join two different lines. But you can do some amazing things at Post Offices—such as buying your TV license or car tax, and collecting your Old Age Pension (Senior Citizen's state pension). Parcel Force is the Royal Mail's express delivery service.

• Deliveries—You can also still have fresh milk and other dairy products delivered to your door. The milk truck (float) comes around very early in the morning, so you don't have to worry about running out of milk for the cereal. More and more supermarket chains are setting up online delivery services, or you can have your shopping delivered to you once you have paid at the checkout. Most people still just take it home themselves, however.

• The cleaners—Again, apart from central London, most cleaners don't stay open too late. Incidentally, these establishments are called "dry cleaners." Although many Brits have their clothes dry-cleaned, the concept of taking regular laundry to the cleaners isn't widespread. People are more likely to do their own laundry, drop a load off at the local Laundromat (Launderette), or have someone come to the house and do it for them. If you stay in a smaller town or village, there may not even be a "cleaners" and you'll have to ask around for the nearest one.

- Help around the house—Domestic help is, not surprisingly, much the same as in the States. While many people call them "cleaners," you'll also hear references to a "daily" and a "charlady" or "char." These are just other names for the person who helps with the cleaning. One thing to remember if you take on such help is that the British iron everything. Try to hide your disbelief when you see your cleaning lady ironing your sheets and towels!

- Another form of help around the house might be a workman, e.g., painter, builder, or utility serviceman. As in the States, you'll be given a time frame of about 10 hours, forcing you to stay in all day—and then they may not show up. When they finally do appear in the UK, though, you will be expected to serve up an endless supply of tea or coffee. Really!

- Beauty—A surreptitious inspection of hands will quickly tell you that manicurists are thinner on the ground than in the United States. A manicure is not quite the priority that it is in the States, and British women in general don't go in for much more than a straightforward manicure. Although talons are popping out everywhere, if you're looking for elaborate nail extensions and live in a small town or village, you may have to venture into a larger town. Men do not have manicures! Most hair stylists will probably have a manicurist on board, but you won't find a separate manicure store on every street corner. Hair salons are just as plentiful as in the States, and just as pricey. When explaining to the hairdresser how you'd like your hair cut, remember that the word "bangs" is totally unknown in the UK. It's your "fringe."

- Cars—If you want your car serviced, mended, or MOT'd (see chapter 6), you'll need to ask for a "garage." They are in plentiful supply, and as in the States, vary in price and quality. It's best to get a few good references before doing business with a particular garage; and if you need to have an MOT test done, the garage has to be authorized to provide this.

  In many garages, if you want to have your car washed, you actually stay in the car while those huge brushes wash and dry it. Great fun, even if you don't have kids, but probably a lawsuit waiting to happen!

- Medical services—One of the first things you'll notice is the different names for everyone and everything in the medical field (see below). Apart from that, British medical services aren't half as scary as is made out in the United States, although they are very different. Doctors and professionals are very much in charge and as a patient you'll be expected to do as you're told. In most cases, you'll need first to register with a local GP (General Practitioner) and then go to him or her with any problem. This is your primary care provider, and you will often be told that you must go to the GP office closest to your home. If need be, the GP will refer you to a specialist. GPs do not refer as many patients to specialists as in the United States and are more willing to give medical advice, probably because they are less likely to incur litigation from their patients. Some GPs still make house calls for extremely sick patients.

  Without getting too boring and technical, Britain has

both state health care (the National Health Service) and private health care. In most cases, this care is provided by the same physicians; you just either get to "jump the queue" in the private system or to choose your own dates for surgery. As an American, your health insurance may give you access to the private system or even an American hospital in the UK. The health care you receive under the NHS (National Health System) differs around the country as the budgets (and therefore the services) are managed at a local level by Primary Care Trusts. In over a decade of taking my kids to the UK, I have sometimes had to pay for the care they receive, and other times it was free because they were under sixteen. Not surprisingly, I am relieving myself of the burden of explaining the system in any greater detail. There are many Web sites and literature in doctors' offices that will supply you with the correct information.

Whether you deliver a baby in a private or NHS facility, you will receive fabulous postpartum (called postnatal) care in the UK. For several weeks after the baby comes home, a midwife or health visitor will come to your home to check on both mother and baby.

Just so you won't be frightened out of your wits the first time you hear this—a doctor's office is referred to as the "surgery," not the office. You will quite often hear references to "surgery times," which means the office hours rather than anything more sinister!

- There is usually no need to make individual searches for specific physicians; most general practitioners' offices provide well women clinics, well baby clinics, and so on, with doctors and nurses specializing in each area. It is not typical to have to visit a number of doctors in different locations unless you are referred on by your GP.

- Dentists—For some reason, most dentists are not addressed as "Doctor" but are simply Mr., Ms., etc. Dentistry is free for children under sixteen and pregnant women; for everyone else there are both NHS-subsidized and private services. Lately it has become extremely difficult to find a dentist taking on more NHS patients. For more complicated dental work, you will usually be referred to a hospital.

  You'll no doubt have heard the jokes about British dentistry and British teeth, and indeed you will see some appalling gnashers while you're over there. It's fair to say that cosmetic dentistry isn't as big as in the States. Most British teenagers would die rather than be seen wearing braces, and teeth just don't seem to be the big priority that they are Stateside (she says, with typical British understatement).

- Opticians—There are optometrists (or ophthalmic opticians) who can test your eyes, and dispensing opticians who can only fit and sell glasses. Like dentists, they are addressed as Mr., Ms., etc, and not as "Doctor." You will find both optometrists and eyeglass stores fairly easily around the UK, although the general public tends to call them all opticians.

- Hotels—London and many of the larger UK cities have all the international hotel chains you'd expect, with approximately the same type of service. If you're planning to travel around the country, however, think *Fawlty Towers*. Not that these hotels are all run by incompetent Basil Fawlty wannabees, but they're about that size, with about that many members of staff. In addition, many of these smaller hotels have no elevator, so make sure you can carry your own luggage up to your third-floor room (fourth floor to you), as there probably won't be a bell hop (porter) either.

Bear in mind that many country hotels were not originally built as hotels. Some were mansions, others were schools and hospitals. Many of them therefore have a labyrinth of corridors and doors to pass through, so be sure to memorize the way from your room to the staircase. If you're a light sleeper, take some foam ear plugs for these hotel visits as many of the room doors are right next to each other and you can often hear your neighbors turning their key in the lock.

Country hotels (as well as bed and breakfasts) are often family-run operations, which means that these people need to sleep! If you arrive at your hotel after closing time, you may well find yourselves either locked out or greeted by an irate hotelier who has just been woken. For the same reasons, these hotels serve breakfast and dinner (not often lunch) at specific times, and there is usually not a 24-hour room service available. In really small B&Bs, the landlady might be prevailed upon to rustle something up between regular dining hours, but you'd better be on your best behavior to accomplish this. The last time I stayed at such a hotel, guests received a room service menu, but when I tried to order a sandwich at 2.30 p.m. I was told I couldn't have one as the chef wasn't due in till 4 p.m.!

If you require a room with two separate beds in it, either state so plainly or ask for a twin room. A double room will get you a room with a double bed in it. If you need to squeeze an extra person in, a cot is not your answer! Friends of mine, traveling around the UK many moons ago, met up with an extra person for one hotel stay. Despite his being well over six feet tall, they insisted that a cot in the room would suffice for the night. The hotel owner tried to protest but was overruled. My friends returned to their room later that night to find a portable crib (baby's "cot" in the UK) set up in the corner of the room. (Ask for a camp bed!)

Here's another funny hotel story I just have to share—even further back in history, two of my husband's colleagues (male and female) checked into a hotel. Since they weren't married, nor even remotely interested in each other, they had booked separate rooms, although the check-in guy didn't look convinced. The woman had somehow managed to sprain her ankle, so about five minutes after departing in the elevator, the solicitous male colleague came back down to the concierge asking for a cane. Smirks and sidelong glances from hotel employees all around. Why? A cane in the UK is called a walking stick. What the guy appeared to be asking for was a cane of the type used for beating people. Should have seen their faces when that slip-up was explained!

- Telephone services—In recent years, British Telecom (BT) has released its stranglehold on the British phone market and there are now numerous phone companies providing service. As in the States, they all offer "unbeatable" packages, so it pays to do your homework before taking the plunge. They also offer Internet service, so again, shop around. If you need e-mail access but not Internet access, there are phones with a small screen and a pull-out miniature keyboard for this purpose. In general, the Brits don't have as many features in their phone service package, so if you need three-way calling, call back, call-waiting, etc., in your home, make sure you tell your service provider. British Telecom provides a free answering service to its customers, as well as the ability to find out whoever called last by dialling 1471. By dialing 141 in front of any number you are calling, you can prevent your number from appearing.

Call waiting—Although the phone companies provide this service, the Brits have not warmly received it. You see, it seems terribly rude to tell one person to wait while you talk to the person on the other line. And then if you have to take the second call, how rude to imply to the first caller that they are not your priority. When it was first available, call waiting was a free service for many people. A large percentage of these people have since dropped it as the etiquette problems were causing ulcers and heartburn. (Just kidding!) Brits are very fond of text messages, so you should probably familiarize yourself before an extended stay in the UK.

One annoying thing you'll notice is the number of people whose phone numbers are unlisted (ex-directory). If you lose someone's phone number in the UK it is often impossible to get hold of them, but you might try this: On my last trip to England, I lost my friends' new address and telephone number and, of course, they were ex-directory. Stumped as to how to contact them, my husband suggested e-mailing them to have them call us—which they did in about five minutes. Most people claim they were forced to go ex-directory because of "dirty" phone calls in the past. I find it hard to believe that such a large percentage of the population could be victims of phone pranks, and suspect that there's a certain cachet to not being in the plebeian phone book.

- Utilities—For gas and electricity there will be a number of companies that can supply you, so once again you should shop around. Don't be alarmed if you never seem to receive a bill—you will be billed quarterly in most cases rather than monthly. Many people have a direct debit payment set up with their banks, and payment via Web sites is available, though less common.

- Trash collection—You'll very quickly learn that the word is "rubbish." Other than the terminology (see below), trash collection is pretty much the same as in the States. Practices vary from one end of the UK to the other, and in some areas the rules can be pretty strict. My mother is only allocated one large trash can (wheelie bin), which must be placed by the side of the road with the two wheels *facing out.* If this is not done, the trash is duly ignored. Additionally, she isn't allowed to put out extra trash, even if it's safely enclosed in a big black trash bag. Whenever she entertains, or has houseguests, she has to ask her neighbors if they have room in their wheelie bins for her extra rubbish. Although most trash haulers won't take large items, you can usually phone your local council office and they'll pick it up for free. Additionally, there are scrap metal dealers in the phone book who will pick it up, or you can take it yourself to the local tip. Most areas now also have additional boxes for glass and paper, which is picked up with the trash.

- Emergency services—If you need to call for an ambulance, police assistance, or the fire brigade, the number is 999.

BRITISH WORDS THAT MIGHT REQUIRE TRANSLATION

Anaesthetist (pronounced "aneesthetist") *n*—anesthesiologist

Antenatal *a*—prenatal

Babysitter *n*—evening caregiver

Building Society *n*—Savings and Loan (although offer many of the same services as banks)

Casualty/ A&E (Accident & Emergency)—ER

Char lady *n*—cleaning lady

Chemist *n*—pharmacist

Cheque *n*—check

Child minder *n*—usually someone who looks after a number of kids after school

Chiropodist *n*—podiatrist

Daily *n*—daily cleaning lady

Deposit account *n*—savings account

Directory inquiries—Information

Engaged (phone) *a*—busy (as opposed to betrothed)

Ex-directory *n*—unlisted phone number

Fringe *n*—bangs

Garage *n*—body shop

Milk float *n*—milk truck

Nanny *n*—full-time baby-sitter

Franked mail *n*—metered mail

Optician *n*—optometrist

Porter *n*—bell hop

Postnatal *a*—postpartum

Sister *n*—head nurse

SRN—State Registered Nurse
Stretcher *n*—guerney
Surface (mail)—overland
Surgery *n*—doctor's office

AMERICAN WORDS THAT THE BRITS DON'T SHARE

Anesthesiologist—anaesthetist (pronounced "aneesthetist")
Bangs—fringe
Bell hop—porter
Body shop—garage
Drugstore—chemist
ER—Casualty or A&E
Guerney—stretcher
OB/GYN—referred to as obstetricians or gynecologists
Optometrist—optician
Overland (mail)—surface mail
Pharmacist—chemist
Podiatrist—chiropodist

RESOURCES

www.nhs.uk—The National Health Service (NHS) Web site. There are links from here to the sites for Northern Ireland, Scotland, and Wales. This site explains the National Health Service for you

www.nhsdirect.nhs.uk—This NHS site provides 24-hour nurse advice and health information, together with a self-help guide to help you "identify symptoms and . . . work out the course of action that is best for you." There is also a phone line offering this service: (0845 4647)

www.usembassy.org.uk—The Web site of the American Embassy in the UK, which gives information about its consulate services for Americans in the UK

www.britishservices.co.uk—A Web site with information about services in your area, both private and public sector

13

Managing with Small Children

RIGHTLY OR WRONGLY, discipline in the UK appears tougher than in the United States. Children are expected to say "Please" and "Thank you" a lot more often and parents are less likely to allow their children to interrupt an adult conversation. You will rarely hear "Is that okay?" tacked on to the end of something said to a child. British parents are also less likely to hold back when encountering bad manners or bad behavior in someone else's child, so don't be taken aback if they demand a "please" before giving your child a cookie (biscuit). They're also not afraid to tell you where you're going wrong in your parenting style. "What he needs is a smacked bottom" is a phrase not unknown to me on my trips back. Children are generally kicked out of the stroller and made to walk at the age of about three.

On the positive side, as one American friend noticed, your social life will revolve less around your kids and more around you and your partner. If invited to dinner, assume it is adults only unless told otherwise. If you can't find a baby-sitter, you'd more likely be expected to decline the invitation than show up with your offspring. As the host, you'll find that the guilt-free joy of inviting someone to dinner without having to dance around the subject of their offspring is very liberating.

Having said all that, you'll be pleasantly surprised by how well children and babies are catered for in everyday life. When my kids were very small, I often brought back items that weren't available in the States; my bounty included individual (scented) diaper trash bags, bendable sun umbrellas, and a sturdy rain cover for my double stroller, long before they debuted Stateside.

In addition:

- Most shopping malls (shopping centers) have excellent and plentiful baby-changing facilities and family toilets, allowing you to get a number of kids plus a stroller in with you. (Bear in mind, the Brits use the word "toilet" for the whole room as well as the receptacle!) There are often toddler seats with straps, allowing you to "see to business" without her making a run for it or trying to see what you're doing at close range.

  I have also experienced the joy of being able to leave my kids at a "crèche" in a few larger stores or shopping centers. These are like day care centers, although you're limited to about an hour in most cases. For a fee, your kids get to play and you get to shop in peace and in the comfort of knowing that they are safe and presumably happy.

- The laws regarding access for the handicapped are much stricter in the UK; this means there is usually excellent access for strollers wherever you go. In many department stores you'll find the usual elevators, stairs, and escalators, but also wheelchair ramps—very useful for strollers, too. Supermarkets have large carts that seat two kids, and their parking lots (car parks) often have special spaces near the store specifically designated for shoppers with young children.

- There are special seats on buses and trains for handicapped passengers and those traveling with small children—these are usually given up by other passengers who see you struggling, and you are within your rights to ask for those seats.

- Although most restaurants now have children's menus, it is still wise to phone ahead to check. You should also do this if you'll need a high chair. There are a great many pubs with excellent play areas (both indoor and outdoor) for kids. Not surprisingly, these are very popular, so if you fancy Sunday lunch at one, get there early to ensure yourself a table.

- Children's menus will be slightly different from what you see in the States. Favorite menu items for British kids are baked beans and sausages, although you'll usually also find fish sticks (fish fingers), chicken nuggets, etc. If your kids can't bear baked beans, make sure you have them omitted from your order, otherwise everything will be "tainted" by them.

- British kids eat a lot of things on toast, which always seems to revolt Americans. I personally love scrambled or poached eggs, or baked beans, on toast but my American kids have yet to see the light. Yours may also voice some resistance, but you might as well be warned that they will be served this concoction at some point. The one British staple that you might want to exercise caution with is Marmite; generally scraped over buttered toast, it is a very salty strong-tasting yeast-extract spread that you definitely have to have a taste for. Kids all over the UK have been raised on Marmite "soldiers" (thin strips of toast) with little or no problems.

- When shopping for your children's clothing, make sure you have their measurements in centimeters, as everything in the UK is now metric. Some clothes are also designated by age, but you'll need the metric information too. Children's shoe sizes are slightly different too, so make sure you have their feet properly fitted before purchasing shoes. British shoe vendors pride themselves on a good fit for your child. Shoe widths go from A to H, and most vendors would rather you bought nothing than a pair of ill-fitting kids' shoes. In addition, friends and family of mine have been known to take shoes back if their kids' feet outgrow a pair too quickly. Based on the promise that there was "ample room for growth," many shoe vendors do not argue with this. Whenever I can, I buy my kids at least one pair of good shoes in the UK. I can always be sure that they will fit perfectly and last longer than they're needed.

- When hiring cars, you can usually rent decent infant and toddler car seats for a set fee for the duration of your car hire. Renting other types of baby equipment, such as a highchair, crib (cot), or stroller (push chair) is not as common as in the States so make these arrangements well in advance.

- Children's parties are sometimes held in the house, but are just as likely to be at some other location with the usual services provided. If you or your kids are invited to a "fancy dress" party, this means a costume party.

- While many children's games and songs will sound familiar, be prepared for some embarrassing moments when you join in the sing-a-longs at school. For instance, the Brits say, "Atishoo, atishoo, we all fall down" at the end of "Ring Around the Rosies" (called "Ring-a-Ring o'Rosies"). The words to "Pop Goes the Weasel" are also totally different until the last line. The "Itsy Bitsy Spider" is often sung as the "Insy Winsy Spider." It might be worth buying an English Nursery Rhymes book just to avoid embarrassing your kids. Tic Tac Toe is known as "Noughts and Crosses" but is played the same way; checkers is called "draughts" (pronounced "drafts"), and chutes and ladders is "Snakes and Ladders."

- Be advised, the song or dance called the "Hokey Cokey" has a chorus in the UK, and things can get extremely physical, if not violent. After "That's what it's all about," the Brits will all join hands and rush into the middle of the circle singing, "Ohhh, hokey cokey" (three times), and then, depending on where you are in the country, a final line. These final lines include: "Knees bent, arms stretched, rah, rah, rah" and "That's what it all about. Oi!" For very small children, the rushing-into-the-middle part can be very frightening, not to mention dangerous.

- Another game you might come across, especially if you have boys, is "conkers." Conkers are extremely hard nuts from the horse chestnut tree. Boys (usually) thread a knotted string through them and then issue conker challenges to their friends and enemies. Basically, one boy lets his conker dangle down (here's where a Brit might say, "As the actress said to the bishop") while the other boy takes aim and tries to smash it with *his* conker. Dangerous for the knuckles. There are various tricks to make the conkers even harder, such as soaking them in vinegar, whiteout, and glue, of all things. If you have a son or two, you'll become familiar with this whole area.

- Dr. Seuss is around in the UK, but not the staple reading of small children as in the States. Don't expect children or adults to join in when you perform your party piece reciting *The Cat in the Hat* in its entirety. Don't expect them to be too impressed, either!

- There is a great natural liquid for colicky babies that I would highly recommend. It isn't easy to get hold of in the United States, but every American I've known who's tried it has been singing its praises ever since. Called "Gripe Water," it is sold in every drugstore (chemist) in the land, and one of its major ingredients is dill seed oil. In most cases it will bring your baby relief and is worth carrying or shipping back to the States when you leave (assuming you still have a baby).

- The term "to bathe" is never used for dumping your kids in the bathtub, and will be greeted with blank looks if used in this context. "To bathe" is used only to describe taking a quick dip in the sea (hence "bathers" for swimwear), although objects could be described as "bathed in sunlight." When washing your kids off in the tub, the verb to use is simply "to bath" them. Incidentally, Brits also say "the bath" rather than "the tub."

- A "babysitter" usually refers to an evening caregiver or someone who's only looking after the children for an hour or so. "Nanny" is more commonly used to describe the person who cares for your child all day. If you're looking for quality child care, try to find someone with a BTEC (Business & Technical Education Council) qualification or someone with a Diploma in Child Care & Education. There are a number of reputable nanny agencies throughout the UK, and many can be found on the Web.

- Registered Child Minders are also available. These people usually look after more than one child in their own home. The law requires that, although not trained in child care, they must have a first aid qualification and undergo a six-week "Introducing Child Minding Practice" course with resulting certification. Make sure they have this certification. The government strictly dictates how many children they can care for (including their own), and the Child Minders are interviewed and inspected by the local authorities annually. See below for government Web sites giving more information and locations of registered Child Minders.

- Something fairly unknown in the United States but very common in the UK is the "leisure center." The nearest equivalent would be a health club, I suppose, but leisure centers offer so much more, usually at a fraction of the price—not least the fabulous soft play areas for children. Most towns have a leisure center within driving distance and in many cases you don't even have to be a member. For a fee and a time limit, kids can run wild and jump about on giant pieces of stuffed play "things." Many leisure centers have swimming pools, too. Parents usually have to stay and watch their kids, but a few centers have attendants to do this. The Brits pronounce "leisure" as "lezher" with a hard "sh" sound.

- A few gems that you'll need to know in order to avoid acute embarrassment are that the rubber thing on the end of a baby's bottle is called a "teat," *not* a nipple; a pacifier is known as a "dummy." Also in the UK, to "nurse" a baby simply means to hold it and cuddle it, so anyone can help out here!

BRITISH WORDS THAT MIGHT REQUIRE TRANSLATION

Babygro' *n*—all-in-one baby outfit
Banger *n*—firecracker (and a sausage)
Beavers—Cub Scouts
Breast-feed *v*—to nurse
Buggy *n*—stroller
Carry cot *n*—bassinette
Clips (for the hair) *n*—bobby pins
Cot *n*—crib
Crèche *n*—day care center
Crib *n*—more like a bassinette on a stand
Dummy *n*—pacifier
Elastoplast (also plaster) *n*—Band-Aid
Fancy dress—costume dress; like children's dress up
Flannel *n*—washcloth
Girl Guide—Girl Scout
Lucky dip *n*—grab bag
Meccano set *n*—Erector set
Mum *n*—Mom
Nappy *n*—diaper
Nurse *v*—to hold or comfort a baby
Nursery *n*—playroom

Nursery school *n*—preschool or day care
Plaster *n*—band-aid
Pram *n*—baby carriage
Pushchair *n*—stroller
Single bed *n*—twin bed
Sledge *n*—sled
Slides *n*—barrettes
Sprog *n*—rug rat
Teat *n*—nipple (on baby's bottle)

AMERICAN WORDS THAT THE BRITS DON'T SHARE

Baby carriage—pram
Barrettes—hair slides
Bassinette—carry cot/crib
Binky—dummy
Bobby pins—clips
Costume party—fancy dress party
Cot—camp bed
Diaper—nappy
Girl Scout—Girl Guide
Grab bag—lucky dip
Nipple—teat
Nurse—to breastfeed
Sled—sledge
Stroller—pushchair
Twin bed—single bed

RESOURCES

www.cache.org.uk—Council for Awards in Children's Care and Education

www.ncma.org.uk—National Child Minding Association's Web site (government-run)

www.childcarelink.gov.uk—Another government Web site to help find child-minding services in England, Scotland, and Wales

14

School's Out

FROM THE GET-GO you'll see that the British and American school systems are very different. For a start, "school" in the UK refers to education from age five through eighteen, and *not* to college or other further education. That is called "college" or "university," and the Brits tend to make a fairly sharp distinction.

What you might not realize is that the *national* education systems within the UK (England, Northern Ireland, Scotland, and Wales) also have their own differences. If you're relocating to Scotland, for example, and have school-age kids, make sure you research the Scottish system rather than the English. (See "Resources" below for relevant Web sites.)

Depending on the age of your child(ren), the duration of your stay in the UK, and what you want to get out of your time there, you should consider carefully whether to go for a British or an American school. Unfortunately, American schools are not exactly dotted all over the country, and are fee-paying, so you may not have a choice. Since British kids attend compulsory, all-day grade school (primary school) from the year of their fifth birthday, *and* start learning to read, write, and do simple math at that age, your child may be slightly behind if in first or second grade. This shouldn't be the end of the world, but you'll want to talk with the school principal (head teacher) before the kids start school, if they're to attend a British school. With older kids (especially when the stay in the UK is only for a year or two), most Americans opt for the American school system to keep them on track when they return to the States. My American friends in England whose kids were preschool age when they settled there have them in an English primary school, which means they shouldn't be behind on their return to the States; plus, they'll have had the cross-cultural experience of attending a "foreign" school into the bargain.

Just so you're prepared:

- Confusingly, in the UK, private schools are "public schools." This is because hundreds of years ago, the religious schools became open to everyone who could pay (hence "public") rather than just to the religious community. The author Evelyn Waugh once said, "Anyone who has been to an English public school will feel comparatively at home in prison." Real public schools are called "state schools" and since there is no separation of church and state, prayers are incorporated into the syllabus. Private grade schools are often called "prep" (preparatory) schools, and the kids are commonly tested in at age four. The Catholic school system is not necessarily fee-paying, but is parochial. Are you with me? (See the vocabulary section below to straighten things out.)

- Compulsory education begins in the child's fifth year, and they usually stay all day. This year is the same as junior kindergarten in many preschools, and is called "reception" in the UK. After that they go into Year 1, which is equivalent to regular Kindergarten. Year 2 is equivalent to first grade, and so on. Schools follow the National Curriculum, which was introduced in the 1990s and is the source of much debate among educators. Many state grade schools (primary schools) have a preschool that is free if you can get a place.

- Unless your child is on the swim team or takes part in some other extracurricular activity, most schools start at 9 a.m. and get out between 3.15 and 3.45 p.m.

- Just a note—the term "gifted" has a much looser meaning in the States. If your child has been in a gifted program while in the United States, Brits will probably be under the impression he or she is a genius, as opposed to simply being of above average intelligence. The term in the UK really refers to extraordinarily intelligent children, and schools on the whole wouldn't have enough of such students to run a separate program for them.

- High school students are legally allowed to leave school at the end of the academic year of their sixteenth birthday. Only a small percentage of the population goes on to "higher education" such as university or technical college. Since many employment opportunities offer high-quality on-the-job training, which is often tied to national vocational exams, there is no great stigma in leaving high school at sixteen. Indeed, it is possible to leave school at this age and become a lawyer, engineer, or accountant through employment-based training and exam success.

- I should point out that even at private schools, the teachers are definitely in charge. Parents are expected to adhere to all the rules and they rarely challenge the curriculum or even the teacher's style. If you're used to having a lot of say in what goes on at your child's school, you might want to hold back and see how it's done first.

- A school uniform is much more common in the UK than in the States, and bears no relation to the *type* of school your kids attend, whether hoity-toity or regular. In most schools, you must purchase the uniforms from a specific retailer rather than just buying any type of navy (gray/green) sweater. Some schools even specify the type and color of PE shoes or indoor shoes. School sports attire is called a "gym kit."

- It's worth noting that the terms "freshman," "sophomore," "junior," and "senior" don't exist either in high school or in college, so if you're explaining how old your kids are, state their ages. The Brits will have no clue if you just name their grades or use U.S. terminology. Since my kids are only in grade school, I still have to count on my fingers when given the grade of a high schooler instead of the age. At college, students are typically called first years, second years, and so on. Students younger than college age are usually known as pupils.

- Many high schools kids take a year off before going to university. This is the "gap" year and it is an accepted part of British academic life; indeed, many people think it a waste not to take this opportunity to travel and experience other cultures before university. I didn't take a year off, and it's one of my biggest regrets since it's much harder to do so once you have secured your place in the rat race.

- High schools and universities in the UK do not have as many ceremonies and rituals as American schools. There are no senior proms, high school rings, yearbooks, Valedictorians, homecoming queens, or honor students. Reunions are becoming more popular, but if you say you are the class of 1936, the Brits probably won't know whether that means you started or finished in that year, and since students can leave at the ages of sixteen, seventeen, or eighteen, it is often very confusing. I recently came across a high school Web site which was using the term "class of " to indicate which year the student *started* there.

- In the British equivalent of the freshman and sophomore years of high school, students take national exams called GCSEs (General Certificate of Secondary Education). These used to be called "O" (Ordinary) levels, and you will hear people use this term even now. In Scotland they are called the Scottish Certificate of Education, Standard Grade exams. Students usually take at least five of these exams, and those hoping to go on to university take between eight and twelve. There are a wide variety of subjects to choose from, although many places of higher education require GCSEs in math, English, one science, and a language, as well as the GCSEs more relevant to the chosen degree course. Students may legally leave high school at the end of the academic year in which they turn sixteen, and many do.

- To attend a university in England, a student must take and pass "A" (Advanced) levels, or "Highers" in Scotland. Again, these are national exams, rather like Advanced Placements, and are taken one or two years after GCSEs. "A" level passes are graded A through E; entrance requirements differ from university to university. More and more high schools in the UK are now offering the IB (Internationale Baccalaureate) program instead of A levels. Applications to universities must be made through a national system called UCAS (University and College Admissions Service). There are tight guidelines and deadlines for applying through this service, so make sure you're well prepped at least a year before your child plans to attend. You are limited to the number of places you may apply for, but should the child fail to meet the entrance requirements for his or her desired university, UCAS has an excellent clearing system and can help get a place elsewhere. (Most high schools will provide sufficient help for students wishing to apply to universities.)

The National Academic Recognition Information Centre for the United Kingdom (NARIC) is a government-run, fee-charging service to help check the comparability of international academic qualifications against UK qualifications. (See below for Web information.)

- Most university degrees take three years to complete; according to the official literature, this is because they are more intensive than U.S. degree courses. Many language degrees and some joint degrees (known as "sandwich courses") take four years. Universities do not run on the semester and "hours" system, and you generally cannot drop in and out like in the States. Basically, you go to university for three (or four) consecutive years (unless there are extenuating circumstances), and you study the same subject the entire time.

There are no majors and minors. If you change your mind about the degree course you are studying, or about the university you are attending, in most cases you have to drop out, reapply for your chosen course or college, and then start all over again. (A bit of a drawback, I will admit.) There are also usually no summer semesters (terms). Postgraduate degrees are often just a yearlong affair. Oxford and Cambridge universities have their own system for naming their terms, as well as their own entrance requirements and exams.

- Some universities have special traditions at the beginning of the academic year. There is no nationally recognized event like Rush, although many universities call the first week "Freshers" week. At my alma mater (also not a known term) we had FAFFY, which stood for "Find a Friendly First Year," but which was really an excuse for the older students to hit on the new ones. Apart from a few high schools (usually private), which may have "houses," there are neither fraternities nor sororities in the UK. If you tell a Brit that so-and-so is your frat brother, you'll probably have to explain the whole frat system as well.

- "Houses" are groups of students within one school; each house has its own teams, which compete against the other house teams. The houses can be named after anything at all—seasons, saints, trees, composers (think Harry Potter—Griffindor, Slitherin, etc.). In some schools the teachers allocate pupils to the various houses, and in other schools existing house members select the new recruits. Where there is a house system in place, however, it is not voluntary as with fraternities and sororities, and you wouldn't find it above high school level.

- The term "101" (when referring to a basic education in any subject) does not exist in the UK. You'll be amazed how many times you'll want to use this phrase, either to make a joke or to explain how simple something is. Refrain—your joke will fall completely flat!

- Another thing you might miss in the British college system is the complete lack of high-profile sports. The Oxford and Cambridge Boat Race takes place every year, and is televised, but don't expect to see your child's varsity team appear regularly even on local television. In addition, most college teams do not have any form of cheerleading.

- A word of warning: If your child takes music lessons in the UK, the terminology is completely, I mean completely, different. Although I am fairly well versed in music terminology, when my daughter started learning violin in the States, I felt like I was learning a whole new language, and to this day am never quite sure of all the note names. Unfortunately, the British names for musical notes bear no relation to the actual value, and are therefore the dickens to remember. A whole note is a semibreve (pronounced "semeebreeve"), a half note is a minim, a quarter note is a crotchet (pronounce the end "t"), and an eighth note is a quaver. They are played in bars, not measures. Steps and half-steps are tones and semitones. The good news is that a music score is read the same way!

- Another warning—history is taught from a slightly different angle. Students learn about the American War of Independence and it is never referred to as the war against the British. Also Americans are not viewed as the winning ingredient of World Wars I and II. If anything, it may be implied that the United States stayed out too long.

Aside from all the technicalities, British school life has a vocabulary all its own, which you'll soon come across if you have a child attending a British school. One day you might be asked to volunteer at the Tuck Shop or the annual jumble sale. We don't want you saying yes when you have no clue what you're getting into, do we?

BRITISH WORDS THAT MIGHT REQUIRE TRANSLATION

Break *n*—recess

Dinner lady *n*—lady who serves lunch and supervises kids at lunchtime recess

Domestic Science—Home Economics

"Gap" year *n*—the year between high school and university which some students take off

Gym shoes *n*—shoes for Phys. Ed. (Find out whether your kid's school specifies type and color)

Head teacher *n*—principal

Hometime *n*—dismissal

Kit *n*—school sports attire

Lollipop man/lady *n*—school crossing guard, so called because of the round stop sign they carry

Playtime *n*—recess

Plimsoles *n*—another name for sneakers

Public school *n*—private school

Pumps *n*—yet another name for sneakers

Reception class *n*—pre-K class

Redbrick universities—older universities, except Oxford and Cambridge

Register *n*—attendance; to take the register
Sandshoes *n*—yet another name for sneakers
Term *n*—semester
Trainers *n*—sneakers
Tuck box *n*—lunch box
Tuck Shop *n*—school candy store
Woodwork *n*—Shop

AMERICAN WORDS THAT THE BRITS DON'T SHARE

Alma mater—the term is not used
Attendance—register; (**take attandance**—to take the register)
Cum laude—doesn't exist
Dismissal—hometime
Fraternity/Sorority—doesn't exist
Hazing—may exist, but the term is not used
Homecoming—doesn't exist
Honor roll—doesn't exist
"101"—doesn't exist
Principal—headmaster/mistress
Recess—playtime; break
Semester *n*—term
Shop—Woodwork
Spelling bee—spelling test
Valedictorian—doesn't exist

RESOURCES

www.nc.uk.net—National Curriculum for England, online. Also links for N. Ireland, Scotland, and Wales

www.ucas.ac.uk—UCAS (Universities and Colleges Admissions Service)

www.hotcourses.com—A service that operates with UCAS and the Department for Education and Skills. It has a large schools database, and can help with searches, applications, and funding for courses in the UK

www.dfes.gov.uk—Department for Education and Skills

www.britishcouncil.org—Official Web site of the British Council, which contains much cultural information and useful links

www.gap-year.com—Everything you need to know about taking a gap year

www.educationuk.org—The Education site run by the British Council

www.naric.org.uk—National Academic Recognition Information Centre for the United Kingdom

www.ukcosa.org.uk—Council for International Education, a service for students (including international) in the UK with many FAQs

www.goodschoolsguide.co.uk—Web site of *The Good School Guide,* which can also be purchased in hard copy. About fifty parents throughout the UK, reporting from a parents' viewpoint about many schools, write on this site, which gives government inspection report information, together with performance statistics. You can search by location or type of school

www.ukonline.gov.uk—The government Web site where you can access information on state schools and their performance statistics; also gives educational parenting tips

www.isis.org.uk—Independent Schools Council Web site offering placement, consultancy, and advisory services to families either in the UK or overseas

www.boarding.org.uk—The UK Boarding Schools Association (BSA) Web site

www.stabis.org.uk—Site of State Boarding Schools Association, where parents only pay boarding fees as the education is free

15

Taking a Vacation

LIKE MOST EUROPEANS, the Brits generally have a healthy attitude toward vacations and usually take at least two consecutive weeks off in the summer. Many people take additional vacations during the rest of the year, and certainly like to travel at the weekend. A four-hour flight from London would get you to Morocco or Moscow, which most Brits might not consider visiting for less than a week. However, since a one- or two-hour flight can get you to many European destinations, more and more people "pop" over to Paris, Amsterdam, Munich, etc., for a day or two.

- People in the UK refer to their vacation as their "holidays." The word "holidays" never refers to Christmas, for example. If you ask people what they are doing for the holidays, they will assume you mean their plans for the following summer. One goes "on holiday," not "on vacation." Note also that the Brits use the plural "holidays" even if they're only talking about one vacation.

- Given the cool summer climate in the UK, many people head for the Continent (the warm bits of Europe!) and beyond. A word of warning—don't leave it till the last minute to book your trip, as tour operators are frequently solidly booked up by then. Many Brits book their holidays up to a year in advance.

- Tour operators (travel agents) can usually provide much cheaper vacation packages than you can put together yourself, but you sometimes take a risk with the facilities when you get there. Stories of half-built hotels have often turned out to be true. Do your homework about the tour operator you choose.

  When choosing an operator, make sure the company holds an ATOL (Air Travel Organizers' Licensing) license, which serves to protect you should your tour operator go bust. It is managed by the Civil Aviation Authority (CAA) and most firms selling air travel in the UK are required to hold this license.

- "Package" holidays are usually run by well-known companies and are available for both high- and low-budget vacationers. The term "package" generally means that your flight and accommodation are booked together and are both included in the price quoted. Sometimes meals are also included—this would be referred to as "all-in." Variations from the travel schedules offered (i.e., flying out of one airport and back to another) are extremely difficult to accomplish, cause major tantrums by the ticketing agent, and always cost more money. A few years ago we took a family holiday to Minorca, the Spanish island, but my husband only came for the first week. This cost him far more than everyone else who stayed for two weeks.

With many UK package deals, you'll be taken to a resort with a lot of other Brits, and unless you go out and search for it, you won't see much of the "real" town or village where you're staying. Very often your accommodation will be exclusively full of people on the same package holiday. "Live entertainment" is a phrase to be wary of, as it can often mean very loud, lackluster local talent playing every night till about 11 p.m. about two feet from your bedroom window. For this reason, you might want to make sure that your accommodation is air-conditioned, as you won't want your windows open.

- A few weeks before the date of departure, many travel agents will post up "last minute deals." If you're lucky, you'll be told your destination, and perhaps even the hotel, but this is often no guarantee of anything more. These holidays have a reputation for being hit or miss in quality. In fact, every summer, there are numerous fly-on-the-wall TV documentaries about the nightmares that holidaymakers face on their package holidays.

- Expect long lines and delays when traveling around the Continent in the summer, especially on charter flights. Many charter flights are scheduled at night, and visitors often arrive at their destination in the early hours of the morning. Fortunately, there will be a courier or rep (tour guide) and a large bus to take you there. If you're traveling on a package deal, flight times are often changed prior to the date, so always confirm flight details before setting off.

Invariably, there is some sort of strike, which will make your journey even more arduous. Continental porters, bus drivers, and the like reserve national strikes for the busiest vacation times, and therefore the hottest times in which to be "queueing," in the summer. Stories of having to wait three or more hours for a taxi at five in the morning (after many hours of air travel) are not exaggerated.

- If traveling "abroad" (outside the UK), check to make sure you don't need any shots before you go. If shots are needed, they are usually required at least a week before the departure date, and for more exotic places, perhaps a few months before. Your travel agent usually knows this, and of course, your local doctor can advise. Also find out whether or not you'll need an entry visa.

- There are topless beaches aplenty on the Continent, and more than you'd think in the UK, too. If this will make you uncomfortable, check with your tour operator before booking a vacation. You'll also quickly notice that Europeans (including the Brits) tend to wear a lot less on the beach than Americans are used to; grown men and little boys often wear Speedo trunks rather than shorts for swimming, and upstanding soccer mom types think nothing of throwing caution, along with their bikini top, to the wind.

- Unlike vacationing within the United States, where you know you'll be able to buy whatever you've forgotten to pack, this isn't always the case when traveling on the Continent or beyond. You should think about taking:

  - Plenty of mosquito deterrents as there are millions of the pests on the Continent.

- An adapter for electrical appliances. Many stores sell adapters for converting British or American appliances.

- Adequate health insurance. Make sure your insurance covers care outside of the UK, and read the small print to check whether you can be flown back in case of hospitalization, or whether you have to remain in the country of your vacation to receive care. Most tour operators can also arrange coverage for you.

- A light jacket or sweater. Typically in Europe, even though it may be extremely hot during the day, the temperature drops significantly in the evening.

- Toilet paper! For packing ease, you might try unrolling the whole thing and packing it in flat folds, although I have recently seen "flat" toilet paper in the stores. Many restaurants in the outer reaches of Europe and beyond still have unpleasant bathroom facilities and little, if any, paper. It is advisable to have toilet paper with you at all times.

- *Never drink the tap water!*

- The UK is currently a rabies-free island and intends to remain so. Do not try to smuggle pets into the UK, as the Pet Travel Scheme (PETS) has very stringent controls and penalties. Animals entering the country from the United States were until recently required to stay in quarantine kennels for six months on proof of rabies vaccination. Now, happily, in most cases your little rabies-vaccinated pooch won't have to endure that. Check with the British

Embassy Web site for the latest information, as there have been some radical changes lately.

BRITISH WORDS THAT MIGHT REQUIRE TRANSLATION

ABTA—Association of British Travel Agents
All-in *n*—all-inclusive (e.g., food and accommodation)
Bucket shop *n*—somewhere you can buy cheap holidays and flights
Charter flight *n*—flight filled entirely with vacationers on a package holiday; you can usually only book these flights along with hotel accommodation
Holiday *n*—vacation
Package holiday *n*—flight and accommodation included
Porter *n*—Skycap
Return *n*—round-trip ticket
Return flight *n*—round-trip flight
Shingle *n*—beach pebble
Single *n*—one-way ticket
Taxi rank *n*—taxi stand
Trolley *n*—luggage cart

AMERICAN WORDS THAT THE BRITS DON'T SHARE

Luggage cart—trolley
Skycap—porter
Taxi stand—taxi rank

RESOURCES

www.defra.gov.uk—Department for the Environment, Food and Rural Affairs Web site, which gives entry and quarantine details. If you search under PETS (Pet Travel Scheme) you will also come across many excellent private veterinarian sites that make the whole thing far more understandable

www.abta.com—Association of British Travel Agents' Web site

www.caa.co.uk—Civil Aviation Authority's Web site, where you will find ATOL information and links

www.aito.co.uk—Association of Independent Tour Operators' Web site, where you'll find great links to other travel sites plus heaps of useful travel information

www.fto.co.uk—The Federation of Tour Operators' Web site. The FTO is a conglomeration of tour operators and airlines, which exists to offer information to the public and address issues. A great source of information about tour operators in the UK

16

Celebrate!

THE THING THAT will definitely make you feel like an outsider is the difference in the holidays celebrated (or ignored) in the United Kingdom. Remember, for a start, that the term "holidays" is used only to refer to vacations. Here are a few things to expect:

- The countries comprising the UK all have their own national holidays, but they usually come and go without much fuss. England has St. George's Day on April 23; Ireland has St. Patrick's Day on March 17 (see below); Scotland has St. Andrew's Day on November 30; and Wales has St. David's Day on March 1. There are also numerous "Bank Holidays" throughout the year, where, yes, the banks are all closed and people generally have the day off work. They differ between the UK countries (England, N. Ireland, Scotland, and Wales) and of course don't coincide with any of the U.S. ones, so best get hold of a national calendar to keep yourself informed.

- Memorial Day, Labor Day, and Thanksgiving will come and go without mention, apart from within American communities. There are a few London hotels that offer Thanksgiving Dinner, but it probably won't be what you're used to. Furthermore, if you're planning to host your own celebrations, start hunting for your ingredients a few months in advance (and you can basically forget about pumpkins unless you're in London).

- Although the UK has a thriving mix of ethnic communities, non-Christian religious feasts, such as Yom Kippur, Ramadan, and the Chinese New Year are not as widely recognized as they are in the States. Since it is specifically an African-American celebration, Kwanzaa is generally not known in the UK.

- Christmas is very big in the UK, and many schools are off for two weeks or more. People tend to stay at home with their families at this time, rather than taking a vacation anywhere. Many traditions surround a British Christmas, such as the Queen's Speech (televised) at around 3 p.m. on Christmas Day. You'll also be treated to mince pies, which are small tarts filled with various baked fruits, and the famous Christmas pud. I would advise taking a very small morsel of this at first, as it is a very thick, rich-tasting pudding that has usually been sitting in alcohol for at least six months. It is often topped with brandy butter to raise your blood alcohol level even further. Oh yes, before I forget—the fruitcake! There'll be an abundance of Christmas cakes around this time. These are fruitcakes, but they are not the joke that they are in the States, and are actually usually moist and delicious. People take a great deal of time and care in preparing their cakes, so the many jokes you may have up your sleeve should perhaps be left for fellow Americans.

Christmas crackers (*not* cookies, by the way) are pulled during dinner, and if they contain paper crowns, you'll find that normally staid Brits think nothing of spending the rest of the meal with these crowns perched precariously on their heads.

- Boxing Day (the day after Christmas Day) is also a Bank Holiday, where no one is expected to go to work; so if you show up at the office, you'll probably be on your own. Boxing Day is often when extended families and friends get together. It is generally agreed that Boxing Day takes its name from the aristocratic practice of making one's servants work on Christmas and therefore allowing them to celebrate the holiday the next day. The family would give their servants and various tradesmen Christmas "boxes." However, the origin of the name is vague and you'll no doubt come across a few variations.

- New Year's Eve ("Hogmonay" in Scotland) is another big event in the UK. Judging by my friends and family, I'd say that most people "have plans" for New Year's Eve, which usually consist of getting together with friends and drinking copious amounts of alcohol. Many of the bigger cities now have outdoor celebrations (yes, in that weather!) and you may even have to have a ticket to attend, as the streets will be closed to non-ticket holders. London has had a New Year's Day Parade for about eighteen years, but in general parades are not part of the British holiday tradition.

In most parts of the UK, "first footing" is a big part of

the New Year celebration, although the finer details vary from region to region. A first footer is literally the first person to cross your threshold in a new calendar year. Where I grew up, the first footer had to be tall, dark, and handsome (naturally) and would carry a lump of black coal. Don't ask me why. In other areas he (it's usually a male) will bring a bottle of whiskey, a loaf of bread, or something else symbolizing prosperity. The first footer knocks at your door, bearing the aforementioned items, and you let him in. People can get very picky about whom their first footer will be.

- Halloween is not quite the huge celebration that it is in the United States, but it is pretty big. Trick or treating is just catching on, and people dress up—but only in scary costumes. If you dress your darling three-year-old as Winnie the Pooh or anything not connected with blood and guts, people will look at you questioningly. At Halloween parties in the UK, you will probably find yourself "bobbing for apples," which basically means dunking your face into a bucket or bowl full of freezing water and trying to catch an apple in your mouth. This tradition seems to be waning in the U.S.

- Easter is quite a big celebration in the UK, and it encompasses a long weekend as both Good Friday and Easter Monday are holidays. Children are given quantities of fairly large chocolate eggs filled with chocolate and candy. These will be available in every store from Valentine's Day. Easter Egg hunts aren't as popular as in the United States, so you won't be able to buy batches of plastic eggs very easily. Where hunts do occur, the eggs will probably be hard-boiled and painted rather than plastic. Around Easter, you will also find delicious Hot Cross Buns. They are to commemorate

Good Friday and are small, sweet sticky buns with currants or raisins inside and a cross made of something sticky on the top. Give them a try!

- Valentine's Day is also celebrated, but cards are usually only sent to the object of your romantic affection. You won't find cards in the stores dedicated to parents, friends, and grandparents. Also, people sending Valentines are not supposed to let the recipient know whom the card is from, and will go to great lengths to disguise their handwriting or will have a friend write a greeting for them. Obviously, a name is not included in the greeting.

    An English friend of mine was once working in the States over Valentine's Day. Many people writing out their Valentine cards were young, single people and she assumed they were sending cards to individuals they were romantically interested in. She couldn't understand why her offers to write out the cards for her friends were all met with puzzled looks and polite declines, until she saw that many were addressed to "Grandma" and "Mom."

- Guy Fawkes Day—One holiday that you've probably never heard of is very big in the UK. On November 5, Brits celebrate Guy Fawkes Day with fireworks and bonfires. Guy Fawkes was a Catholic rebel who hid barrels of gunpowder under the House of Lords in November 1605, hoping to ignite them during the opening of Parliament, which the Protestant king James I was to attend. The plot was discovered and the tragedy avoided. Fawkes was burned at the stake in 1606, and ever since, people have made effigies of him (called a "guy"), which are placed atop a bonfire and burned on November 5. You may also encounter small children lugging around a stuffed effigy asking for "a penny for the guy." Guy Fawkes Day is also known as Bonfire Night.

- April Fool's Day (April 1) is very big in the UK. Pretty much every year a national joke is played by one television channel, radio station, or newspaper proclaiming anything from haggis growing on trees to an imminent landing from outer space. Someone you know will either be the prankster or the victim on April Fool's Day. Please note, however, that it all has to end at noon, or you'll look like the fool!

- Red Nose Day is another one you've probably never heard of, but it is now *huge* in the UK. Launched on the good old BBC television channel in 1988, the campaign has raised well over £220 million to help various causes both in the UK and in the world's poorest countries. Red Nose Day is organized by Comic Relief, a group of famous (primarily) British comics, and helped by national and international celebrities. Red Nose Day happens in the spring, every two years (odd years), when millions of normally staid British people walk around wearing red plastic noses. The red nose differs slightly with each Red Nose Day; examples have included noses with arms, furry noses, and squeaky ones. All proceeds benefit the Comic Relief causes. The day culminates in various TV extravaganzas and lots of money is raised.

  Incidentally, there is a U.S. Comic Relief, founded in 1986 and headed by Robin Williams, Whoopi Goldberg, and Billy Crystal. It has raised millions for homeless people in the United States, but sadly, Red Nose Day hasn't been picked up.

- In Scotland, Burns Night is celebrated on January 25. Robert Burns (1759–1796) was a prolific Scots poet, particularly famed for penning "Auld Lang Syne." The food eaten at this celebration includes powsodie (sheep's head broth) and the famed haggis (minced mutton, offal, oatmeal, and spices boiled in a sheep's stomach), so make sure to eat beforehand!

- St. Patrick's Day, although recognized in the UK, is not the extravaganza that it is in the States. When I was little, it was definitely a holy day, and in general even now the Catholic schools might get the day off, but there are no wild parties or green bagels to be found!

- There is no Groundhog Day in the UK; indeed, most people won't even know what a groundhog is.

- Pancake Tuesday or Shrove Tuesday, is the same as Fat Tuesday, but let me warn you that the Brits will die laughing when they hear you say the American name! Sometimes you will see pancake races, in which not only do the contestants have to race holding a pancake in a skillet, but there is usually the requirement that the pancake be tossed at least three times before the finish line. British-style pancakes are more what Americans would call crepes, and are usually eaten with a sweet filling on Pancake Day.

- Remembrance Day—or Poppy Day, as it is also known, is like Memorial Day in the States, only it is held on the Sunday closest to November 11 each year. Bright red paper poppies are sold to raise funds for war veterans, and worn like small corsages by everyone in remembrance of the fields in Flanders where battles were fought during World War I. The Poppy Appeal helps fund the Royal British Legion, which in turn contributes to the welfare of ex-servicemen and women and their families.

- Parties in general can bring a few surprises: If you invite people to a "cookout," the Brits will have some idea that there's food involved, but that's about the limit. They might even make the connection to cooking outside, but you'd be safer calling it a BBQ. Similarly, a "potluck" will ring no bells whatsoever, so better to explain that guests are supposed to bring a dish. Tailgating is generally not done in the UK, so don't even bother trying to organize this type of party. If you find yourself invited to a "fancy dress" party, it means a costume party, and most people will get into the spirit and dress up. If you're invited to a themed party, you might want to ask your host if people will be dressing up. The Brits use any excuse to be silly and dress up!

- When you receive a party invitation, you are expected to RSVP as soon as possible. Leaving it till a day or two before the event is considered incredibly rude (not to mention inconvenient for the host). If you're sending out invitations, don't be afraid to call people who haven't responded. If you want people to bring a bottle, the abbreviation is usually PBAB (Please bring a bottle) rather than BYOB, which, having no "please" in it, would be seen as rather rude.

Incidentally, lest you bring scorn and derision upon yourself from the nearest Brit, the request for someone to RSVP requires no "please" after it, as it is already included in the abbreviation (Répondez, s'il vous plait).

17

Weddings, Funerals, and Everything In Between

CHRISTIANITY (specifically the Church of England) is the established religion in the UK; therefore, I have based this chapter on typical Christian services and customs. The UK is, however, a country rich in ethnic and religious diversity, and there is every possibility that you will have the opportunity to attend a non-Christian ceremony.

Churches often get very picky about who can use them for weddings and christenings. Many churches refuse people who are not regular attendees and no amount of a "donation" will change this. Indeed it may put the minister's back up even further. Funerals do not seem to be subject to this rigidity however.

WEDDINGS

Though they may look similar, weddings in the UK are very different from U.S. weddings. Since you're meant to be on your best behavior, it goes without saying that there is huge potential to embarrass yourself or your hosts, sometimes without even realizing it. The first time I went to an American wedding, I looked at the guy standing at the top of the aisle and wondered why he was pointing his elbow at me. Since I was very new to the States, I decided that there could be any number of reasons, and walked straight past him, leaving my husband apologizing profusely to the confused groomsman! You can also expect some crucial differences regarding funerals and christenings, so read on.

- The riotous parties that take place some time before the actual wedding are called "stag nights" and "hen parties." You might see a bride-to-be on her hen night wearing a ridiculously huge paper top hat adorned with flowers, ribbons, toilet paper, or whatever her friends could find.
- Engagement rings are very often not solitaires. The Brits typically go in for clusters, usually a sapphire, emerald, or ruby with diamonds as a surround. There is no "rule" about the ring having to cost three months' salary. As for anniversary rings, the good news is that you don't have to wait ten years to get one. They are called "eternity" rings in the UK and are often given after the birth of the first child, although this is not a hard and fast rule.
- Wedding invitations do not usually include a response card; you are expected to write your own response letter. American-style invitations are becoming more common,

but usually, the higher up the social ladder, the plainer the wedding invitation.

- Showers are not typical in the UK, and the term is still not widely known, although as an American, you can get away with hosting one and your guests will be delighted. Just be prepared to have to talk them through it! If you're an American bride (or mother-to-be) in the UK, don't be offended if no one throws you a shower—it's just not part of the wedding culture. Similarly, weddings do not include a rehearsal dinner or a bridesmaids' breakfast.

- If the wedding is to be in a church, the "banns" must be read beforehand. This is a centuries-old tradition whereby your intention to marry must be posted in or outside the church for the three Sundays before your intended wedding date. This was so that, in days of poorer record keeping, anyone knowing of any reason why you shouldn't lawfully marry (e.g., already married) could have a quiet word with the priest or vicar. The Church of England has recently been seeking to replace the banns with a less formal "welcome" announcement by the church.

- Marriages may either take place in a church or a venue approved by the General Register Office. Open-air venues are not included in the approved list. Visit the GRO Web site for information on legal requirements and approved venues.

- Most weddings take place earlier in the day than in the States, and are followed by a sit-down, formal dinner. There is often a gap between this and a less formal dance in the evening, where additional guests may be invited. Guests at such a wedding are required to amuse themselves for the duration between the day and evening event, although some weddings just keep on going through to the evening part. The last English wedding I went to started at 2.30 p.m. and went straight through till midnight.

- Friends and/or family generally do not sing at each other's weddings. Although I have been to a few British weddings where a semi-professional singer has performed, solo artists are not yet the norm. If you're a singer and want to offer your services to a British friend for his/her wedding, be prepared for a cool, even baffled response. Many churches offer their local choral services for weddings but I would advise you to listen to them before taking up this offer!

- Black tie is not usual attire for weddings, even for the wedding party—and even if the wedding takes place later in the day. (I do hear, however, that this trend is growing.) Morning jackets or regular suits are worn. In general, female guests do not wear evening attire, even if the wedding is later in the day. If there is to be an evening dance, a change of clothes is appropriate. Be prepared for a plethora of big hats worn by the female guests.

- There are usually fewer bridesmaids than in American weddings, and they are not matched by an equal number of groomsmen. If you are asked to be a bridesmaid by a British bride, you will usually not be required to pay for your own dress. If you are an American bride asking Brits to be bridesmaids, they will not expect to have to pay for their own dresses! If you are asked to be the chief bridesmaid, that's the maid of honor role, but there's usually nothing extra to do on your part, other than help the bride. By the way, the phrase "to stand up at someone's wedding" has no particular meaning in the UK—in fact, "to stand up for someone" means to defend them in an argument.

So, if you are having Brits as part of your wedding party, be very specific when approaching them about it.

- Bridesmaids and groomsmen do not flank the altar as here. Bridesmaids usually sit or stand behind the bride in the first row, and groomsmen (ushers) sit with the groom. In most cases, the bride's "people" sit on one side of the aisle and the groom's on the other. Mothers, aunts, and grannies make their own way to their seats and there is no ceremony involved in this. In fact, female guests do not have to wait to be escorted to their seats by groomsmen. If they do so, they will probably receive strange looks and still be standing there when the bride comes down. At the end of the ceremony, guests are less organized as they exit the church. Basically, once the bride and groom have made their exit, it's an orderly free-for-all.

- The bride and father (or escort) usually go straight from the house to the back of the church and then proceed immediately to the altar. There is often no opportunity even to check your hairdo on the way, and the bridal party is rarely able to dress at the church before the ceremony. In many neighborhoods around the UK, local people gather to watch the bride leaving the house for her wedding. When I was little, the bride's father threw out pennies as the car was pulling away and the children all scrambled to collect the loot. The bride and escort always walk down the aisle in front of the bridesmaids. Bridesmaids typically walk down the aisle in pairs, immediately behind the bride.

- It is considered slightly tacky to take pictures in the church during the actual ceremony, and is often specifically prohibited.

- The wedding party usually has the official photos taken in full view of their guests, rather than disappearing for an hour and leaving the guests to fend for themselves.

- The wedding reception is usually more formal, with speeches by the bride's father, the best man, and the groom. Other guests do not typically make speeches. (If you're required to make a speech, there are many "wedding etiquette" books in the stores.) If the garden of the bride's parents is large enough, and weather permits, the wedding reception is often held in a large, fancy tent called a marquee. It is also quite common to have a toastmaster guide the proceedings at a wedding reception. The toastmaster wears a bright red jacket and carries a gavel. His job is to inform guests when to go through to dinner, to announce the bride and groom, and so on.

- You'll be horrified to learn that most British wedding cakes are fruitcakes, covered with rock-hard icing. Indeed, the bride and groom can rarely cut into it at the reception. Many Americans, on trying these cakes, are pleasantly surprised at how much better they taste than the American version (which wouldn't be difficult). British fruitcakes are steeped in alcohol, therefore very moist and tasty (in my opinion). Traditionally, the top layer of the cake is stored and used as the christening cake for the firstborn. Don't worry if you are ever offered a piece of christening cake—the alcohol preserves everything.

At the cake-cutting part of the reception, British couples merely cut into the cake (if they can) and let the caterers do the rest. They do not "feed" each other a piece, but simply pose for a few photos. British brides also do not toss the bouquet backward, nor does the groom try to remove any item of clothing from the bride—at least at the reception!

- Clinking glasses during the wedding reception is a call for someone to make a speech in the UK, so be careful when you do this as you could turn a wedding reception into a very long-winded affair.
- And finally, a word of warning about weddings—there is no unwritten rule in the UK that you have up to a year after the wedding in which to buy the happy couple a gift. If your gift doesn't materialize within a short time afterward, it will appear rude. As in the States, couples often organize lists at various department stores in town where you can purchase a gift.
- Wedding anniversary celebrations in the UK are often big social affairs, especially for silver (25 years), ruby (40), gold (50), and diamond (60). If invited to one of these, you are expected to take a gift, unless otherwise directed. Typically, a couple celebrating a silver wedding anniversary will receive lots of silver gifts.

FUNERALS

- Although the whole concept is obviously the same, a few things might take you by surprise. In general nowadays, once a person dies, they are taken off by the undertaker and then placed in a chapel of rest until the service. You may view the body at the chapel, but there might not be anyone else there at the same time, and there certainly won't be any kind of reception around an open coffin. The word "wake" still has Irish connotations and suggests a rip-roaring, usually very alcoholic send-off for the deceased.
- Funeral services generally follow a typical religious order of

service, with much less involvement by the deceased's friends and family. Although they might do a few of the readings, the concept of friends and relatives making speeches about the deceased is catching on, but still not quite what it is in the States.

- After the funeral service, friends and family either go to the cemetery for the burial or to the crematorium for another short service. At the cemetery, there probably won't be a carpeted area with awning; you'll simply stand around the hole in the ground and often will watch the coffin being lowered into the ground. At the crematorium, after another brief service, you might see the coffin being wheeled off to goodness knows where; if you're lucky, a curtain will simply be closed in front of it. You'll probably find both options a little more traumatic than the American equivalent.
- After this, there is usually a reception at a family member's house, although it is becoming more and more common to hold the reception in a private room somewhere.
- Most attendees still wear dark clothing to funerals.

CHRISTENINGS

- Christenings differ, depending on the denomination of the baby in question. In general, Catholic babies have fewer godparents than Protestant kiddies. In fact, the only christenings I have been to where the godparents numbered more than four were all Protestant services.
- Depending on the individual church, christenings can be either part of the regular Sunday service, or a private affair outside of regular service hours. Some churches give you

the choice and others do not. Similarly, in some churches a fee will be charged and in others it's all free.

- As with funerals, a reception is held after the service. These are typically held at the parents' home, but more and more are being held at an outside venue. A christening cake is made, again usually fruitcake. This is often the top tier of the parents' wedding cake which has been re-iced.
- Gifts are usually bought for the baby—normally small keepsakes of a religious nature.

BRITISH WORDS THAT MIGHT REQUIRE TRANSLATION

Banns *n*—the posting of the wedding announcement at the church, three weeks before the wedding date

Chief bridesmaid *n*—maid of honor

Bottom drawer *n*—hope chest

Hen party *n*—bachelorette party

Marquee *n*—large tent

Stag party *n*—bachelor party

To stand up for someone *v*—to defend someone verbally

RESOURCES

www.forbetterforworse.co.uk—A wedding site that lists available venues, as well as information about the legalities of getting hitched in the UK

www.gro.gov.uk—General Register Office's official Web site

18

The World of Work

ON THE SURFACE, work life seems fairly similar in the UK—the offices look the same, although not as many are air-conditioned. One noticeable difference between British and American working women, however, is footwear. British women would not be seen dead in a work suit and sneakers. So, if you don't want to flag yourself as an American in town, either wear regular flat shoes and change at the office, or make sure you can walk around in your chosen office shoes.

Office *culture* is somewhat different, and that is what Americans notice most.

- Finding a job—In the United States, word of mouth is used a lot when job-hunting, but in the UK, job vacancies are often advertised in daily newspapers or handled by recruitment companies. It is far less common to acquire a position because someone has put in a good word for you or just happens to know of a vacancy. You might even find someone is visibly uncomfortable if you ask him or her to make an introduction for you.

When job-hunting, you will be asked to submit your CV (curriculum vitae), which is your résumé.

- The Brits draw a sharp distinction between being fired (sacked) and being let go for any other reason. "Getting the sack," or being fired, would mean that the employee had done something fairly egregious at work, since oral and written warnings must ordinarily be given before anyone can be fired. When employees are let go due to financial problems or restructuring in the organization, this is usually termed "being made redundant," and has much less stigma attached. If you know someone who's been made redundant, don't offend him or her by using the "f " (fired) word. Incidentally, the term and the concept of "employment at will" do not exist in the UK.

- Since many work-related "benefits," such as health insurance, have traditionally been provided by the state, British workers may not recognize the term "benefits." If you're asking what the employment package is, be specific and ask about health insurance, pension plans, etc. If you're pregnant and employed under a British contract, maternity leave provisions are government mandated and very generous.

- Equipment—You'll find you may have to chuck most of your office equipment once in the UK. Most ring binders are two-hole binders, so if you want to take along your three-ring ones, make sure you also take your three-hole punch. Paper is a different size and gets called by different names. Unfortunately, American letter size is slightly smaller than the UK equivalent (called foolscap or A4), and doesn't fit into their faxes, binders, or envelopes. Transferring documents from one computer to another is also a problem as the page lengths and setups are different. Best to get someone who's really good with the word processing side of things to help you out there.

- You'll find a lot of "diaries" in the workplace. It's not that everyone's busy capturing their thoughts and memories on paper; that's the word used for a calendar. When asked if he can attend a meeting next Tuesday, a person might say, "I'll check my diary and get back to you." A calendar is usually much larger and hangs on the wall.

- When word processing in the UK, remember that spelling is often different. If the recipient will be a Brit, you should run the document through a British English spell check. Although Brits are aware that Americans use "z" where they would place an "s" (e.g., organize), there are many more spelling differences of which both Americans and Brits are initially unaware, such as defence/defense for the noun. We don't want your prized presentation material to look sloppy, now, do we?

- Writing the date can cause no end of confusion as the Brits write down the day, followed by the month, rather than the month first. My birthday—September 4—becomes 4/9. It will take you months if not years to change over, but change you must unless you want to miss meetings and bounce checks all over the place. When in doubt, write the month out in full.

- Meals—Although many people eat a sandwich on the go at lunchtime, most eat breakfast at home. In general, the Brits do not grab a coffee and doughnut on the way into their office building. Apart from London, few cities and towns have breakfast places, other than McDonald's and Wendys. In many workplaces, there is the delightful "tea trolley," which is wheeled in around midmorning and/or mid-afternoon, and is laden with cakes and biscuits as well as huge pots of tea.

- Many companies have their own cafeteria (often called the "canteen"), where the food is either free or subsidized. While "liquid lunches" are far less common than they used to be, it is still somewhat acceptable to have an alcoholic drink at lunchtime. Some companies expressly forbid it, if the worker would put people at risk by having even one drink—forklift truck drivers, people in charge of children, and transport workers being obvious examples.

- Professional terms are also often different. For example, the term "CPA" is not known; its equivalent is a chartered accountant. "Attorney" is not much used (and is spelled "attourney") since the British legal profession is divided into barristers and solicitors, depending on which courts they appear in. (Barristers appear in higher courts.) In Scotland, barristers are known as advocates. Corporate attorneys are usually called solicitors; and there are no such things as paralegals. Realtors are known as estate agents, and doctors are rarely called physicians.

- Office jargon is just as rife but some doesn't translate very easily. As we saw earlier, avoid using sports analogies and phrases when speaking to British co-workers as the meaning is almost guaranteed to be skewed, if not completely lost. Many Americans use sports terms so often in speech that they don't even think of them as sports related. In case you're one of these, "touch base," "step up to the plate," and anything to do with left field are all sports-based phrases that may confuse Brits. The Brits will also jump in with their own jargon, which you should question as soon as it starts going over your head. One example is "ticking all the boxes." Since the Brits say "tick" instead of "check," this phrase means checking yes to everything that should have been done; in short, meeting all one's objectives.

- To "table" a topic in the UK means to put something on the agenda, rather than to adjourn the discussion until the next time—another instance where you could get completely the wrong meaning in a very important meeting.

- The verb "to revise" also causes many problems. Typically, "to revise" in the UK means to study for an exam, and "revision" describes that activity. Brits would understand you using "revision" to mean a change in something, but I advise you to check that this meaning has been communicated.

- When writing letters in the UK, the rule is "Dear Sir . . . Yours faithfully" and "Dear Mr. Smith . . . Yours sincerely." When you don't know the person's name, use "Yours faithfully," and if you know the person's name, use "Yours sincerely." I remember this rule because the S's (Sir and Sincerely) *don't* go together. If you don't know whether the recipient is male or female, the salutation is "Dear Sir or Madam." Letters, especially in business, would not usually conclude with "Sincerely" or "Best regards" unless you had developed a personal relationship with the addressee. E-mail correspondence is thankfully, less formal and rigid.

- Acronyms provide a whole new language for you to learn. It's not so much that the acronyms mean different things, but that the Brits use totally different acronyms altogether:

  AOB—Any other business

  NB—Short for the Latin *Nota bene*, which you will actually hear some people say. It means literally "Note well," and is used frequently in any type of documentation to draw particular attention to something.

POETS day—Friday (Piss Off Early, Tomorrow's Saturday), obviously not written in anything remotely official!

PTO—Seen at the bottom of a page, means "Please turn over."

OTT—Not really just an office acronym, but while we're on the subject . . . this means "Over the top" and is used to describe anything from someone's plunging neckline to over dramatic behavior or a flashy car.

TTFN—Ta ta for now.

BRITISH WORDS THAT MIGHT REQUIRE TRANSLATION

Biro *n*—Bic-type pen

Blue tack *n*—sticky putty that leaves no marks on the wall

Boiler suit *n*—coveralls

Brackets *n*—parentheses

Bulldog clip *n*—larger black paperclip

Canteen *n*—cafeteria

Chartered accountant *n*—CPA

CV (curriculum vitae) *n*—résumé

Diary *n*—calendar (also means journal)

Drawing pin *n*—push pin/thumb tack

Felt pen/Magic Marker *n*—Sharpie

Foolscap *n*—almost letter-size paper

Full stop *n*—period

Gaffer *n*—boss

Hash sign *n*—# pound sign
Leaving "do" *n*—someone's leaving party
Notice board *n*—bulletin board
Oblique *n*—slash
On the dole—to be unemployed
Pink slip *n*—papers received when fired
Pound sign *n*—pound sterling sign (£)
Rubber *n*—eraser
Sacked *a*—fired
Sellotape *n*—sticky tape
Skive (off) *v*—to play hookey or to shirk work duties
Skiver *n*—someone who either doesn't pull their weight or
    who misses work a lot
Stroke *n*—slash
Tick *n or v*—check
Typex (pronounced "Tippex") *n*—whiteout
Venue *n*—meeting place
Wastepaper basket *n*—trash can for paper only

AMERICAN WORDS THAT THE BRITS DON'T SHARE

Calendar—diary
Check—tick
Coveralls—boiler suit
Fired—sacked
Grandfathered—not a known term
Graveyard shift—night shift
Meeting place—venue
Pound sign—hash sign

Push pin—drawing pin

Résumé—CV (curriculum vitae)

Sharpie—felt pen/Magic Marker

Slash—oblique/stroke

Sticky tape—Sellotape

Thumb tack—drawing pin

Trash can—wastepaper basket/bin

Water cooler—water fountain (not a feature in British workplaces)

86 it—not used

19

Attire and Accessories

CLOTHING IS ONE AREA where you'll definitely be faced with strange terminology and a few odd customs. Most confusing is the fact that Brits and Americans use the same names for different things. A vest in the UK is the undergarment worn on the top half of the body; a waistcoat is the name used for a vest. What you're not often told about are the unspoken rules governing dress. In Chicago in the winter, guests entering my home almost always remove their shoes at the door, despite my assurances that it's okay to leave them on. In the UK, this wouldn't be expected and you might even make your host a tad uncomfortable if you pad around in your socks.

- There is no unwritten rule in the UK about when you may wear white shoes, linen, velvet, or anything else, for that matter. Since the temperature is fairly mild all year round, anything goes. What the Brits tend not to do is decorate themselves according to the season or holiday. You'll rarely see adults adorned with Christmas-themed sweatshirts or Valentine-embellished attire, so watch out for the sidelong glances when you wear your collection!

- It does not cause great alarm when women don't wear hose. As long as the legs are fairly tanned, it's okay, although you'll probably see some ghastly white specimens too. Businesswomen also go hoseless in the summer. Talking of hose, women tend not to wear the baked bean color that is common in the United States, nor do they wear white or cream pantyhose (tights) unless it's part of a nurse's uniform. Actually, the world of hosiery gets a tad complicated. "Stockings" only ever refer to hose that go up to the thigh and require extra equipment to keep them up. These extra pieces are called suspenders and the garter belt goes around the top of one thigh, although it is rarely worn except by men dressing up as women. Regular hose are (is?) tights. American suspenders are known as braces in the UK—stay with me now!

- The world of underwear can also be a bit of a minefield, and bears repeating. "Pants" refers to underpants (men's or women's) and not to trousers. Ladies wear knickers, not panties. What Americans would call knickers are known as either knickerbockers or plus fours in the UK and generally not worn, even for golf. Slang names for underpants include skivvies, undies, and smalls.

- Shoe sizing in the UK is different, and the Continent is different again. As a rule, a woman's size in the United States will be two sizes smaller in the UK. An 8.5 in the United States is about a 6.5 in the UK and a 39/40 on the

Continent. I would advise having children's feet measured professionally at first.

- Clothes sizing (for women) is also different. If you're an 8 in the United States, expect to go for at least a 12 in the UK—jump up two sizes. (Many retailers might tell you it's only one size difference, but believe me, if you're an 8 in the U.S. you won't fit into a 10 in the UK.) I also often find that British clothes are less generous in the hips and thighs, so try stuff on before you buy it. Children's clothes are marked in age and in centimeters.

- Mothers and daughters rarely, if ever, wear matching outfits, so again, be prepared for looks of disbelief if this is your thing. In addition, grown women never wear jumpers, probably because they are often part of a little girl's school uniform (referred to as a "pinafore") and therefore have a strong association with children. Incidentally, "jumper" is the word for "sweater" in the UK.

- The clothes you'll wear in the rain (and there will be lots of them) require special attention, as some of the words are almost unbelievable. A raincoat will be referred to as a "mac" (proper name "Mackintosh"); a slightly padded raincoat will be an "anorak" (not as thick as a parka); and a rain slicker that packs into its own pocket is a "cagool." Your rubber, rainproof boots are your "wellies" (proper name "Wellington boots"); the hat you might wear is your "Sou' Wester," and your "galoshes" are your rubber overshoes, although they are less common in the UK than one would imagine. Oh yes, and you'd be well advised to carry a "brolly" (umbrella) with you at all times.

- Many brand names that are everyday words in the United

States are simply not known in the UK. Examples include Mary Janes, Birkenstocks, Docksiders, and penny loafers.

- Just so you don't *really* embarrass yourself—a bikini refers to a woman's two-piece swimsuit and is never used to refer to men's underwear. A thong is a skimpy piece of underwear and never used to refer to footwear—those are "flip-flops."

BRITISH WORDS THAT MIGHT REQUIRE TRANSLATION

Anorak *n*—padded rain jacket

Badge *n*—button

Balaclava *n*—ski mask–type hat, covering entire face except mouth and eyes

Bathers *n*—swimsuit (from bathing suit)

Boiler suit *n*—coverall

Bowler hat *n*—Derby

Box *n*—sports cup

Braces *n*—suspenders

Brooch (rhymes with "coach") *n*—pin

Brolly *n*—umbrella

Bum bag *n*—fanny pack

Cagool *n*—thin, wind/rain proof jacket

Court shoes *n*—pumps

Cardie/cardigan *n*—sweater that either zips or buttons up the front

Cossie/cozzie *n*—swimsuit (from swimming costume)

Cravat *n*—Ascot

Cuff *n*—turn-up at the end of a sleeve

DJ (dinner jacket) *n*—tuxedo

Dressing gown *n*—robe

Dungarees *n*—overalls

Flip-flops *n*—thongs

Frock *n*—dress (old-fashioned wording)

Garter (belt) *n*—fancy piece of elastic, worn round the top of the leg with stockings; the item the groom removes at a U.S. wedding!

G string *n*—thong underwear

Handbag *n*—purse

Hush Puppies *n*—a brand name; very comfortable shoes

Jersey *n*—sweater

Jesus sandals *n*—simple leather sandals with one strap across the toes and another at the ankle

Jimjams *n*—pajamas (UK spelling is "pyjamas," by the way)

Jumper *n*—sweater

Knickers *n*—ladies' panties

Ladder *n*—run (in hose)

Mackintosh (Mac) *n*—raincoat

Off the peg—off the rack

Overalls *n*—coveralls

Pants *n*—underpants

Pinafore *n*—jumper

Pinny *n*—apron

Plimsoles *n*—sneakers

Plus fours *n*—knickers

Polo neck *n*—turtleneck

Pop socks *n*—knee high hose

Press studs *n*—snap fasteners

Prêt-à-porter *n*—ready-to-wear

Pumps *n*—sneakers

Purse *n*—wallet

Sandshoes *n*—light children's sneakers, like Keds

Smalls *n*—panties, underwear

Stockings *n*—thigh-length hose that require garters, etc.

Sou'wester *n*—rainproof hat with large flap at back (think
    Paddington Bear)

Suspenders *n*—garters

Thong(s) *n*—G-string underwear

Tights *n*—hosiery (thick or thin)

Trainers *n*—sneakers

Trilby *n*—fedora

Turn-ups *n*—cuffs (on trousers)

Twin set *n*—sweater set

Vest *n*—undergarment

Waistcoat *n*—vest

Wellington boots (wellies) *n*—rubber rainproof boots

AMERICAN WORDS THAT THE BRITS
DON'T SHARE

Ascot—cravat

Barrette—hair slide

Button—badge

Cuffs (on trousers)—turn-ups

Cup (sports)—box

Derby—bowler hat

Dop kit—toiletries bag

Fedora—Trilby

Garter—suspenders

Jumper—pinafore

Knickers—plus fours
Mary Janes—the name is not known
Off the rack—off the peg
Panties—knickers, briefs, smalls
Pin—brooch
PJs—jimjams; pyjamas
Pocketbook—handbag
Pumps—court shoes
Purse—handbag
Rain slicker—cagool
Robe—dressing-gown
Sneakers—trainers
Suspenders—braces
Sweater—jumper, jersey
Thongs—flip-flops
Tuxedo—DJ (dinner jacket)
Vest—waistcoat
Wallet (ladies)—purse

20

Crime and Violence

ONE THING MANY AMERICANS living in the UK appreciate is the marked decrease in violent crime. Handguns are still fairly rare, homicides make national headlines, and incidents like school massacres happen about once a decade, if that. Also seemingly less common is child abuse by caregivers, telephone cons, etc. Don't be lulled into a false sense of security, however, since the UK has one of the highest per capita rates of theft in Europe.

In this chapter I'll give you an idea of what to expect in terms of the crimes you might be susceptible to while in the UK, as well as translate for you some of the more colorful words in the criminal lexicon.

- Since people all over Europe have been living with the threat of terrorism for decades, there is, even now, a higher level of security awareness than in the United States. Look around the larger tube and train stations in London—no trash cans. If you leave your bag or suitcase unattended even for a second, it will be whisked off and "detonated" before you know it's gone. Similarly with unclaimed luggage left on the carousel—expect to find the airport terminal evacuated when you come back for the suitcase you left behind!

- Statistics show (and personal experience tells me) that you're much more likely to have your car and/or house broken into in the UK. Always lock all doors and windows when you leave the house either at night or during the day. If your door has a glass pane close to the latch, burglars think nothing of smashing the pane, thrusting their hands in and letting themselves in. Fortunately, most British homes are well armed against burglary attempts. Many Brits don't even sleep with their bedroom windows open unless they have top windows that are too small for a human to squeeze through. If living in a house in the UK, check the insurance policy; some insurers will not cover you if it is discovered that your alarm wasn't switched on when the house was burglarized (burgled).

- Always lock your car and never leave valuables on display. Some people have car radios that can be removed when the car is parked, and many people have locks (called Krooklocks) over the steering wheels. Most thieves can disable a car or house alarm but are put off by visible deterrents such as steering locks in the car, lights on in a house, barking dogs, etc. House burglars are usually unarmed, petty thieves, and can often be scared off with a loud scream!

A few years ago I heard a charming story on the local radio in England. A woman, taking her son to the doctor's office, stopped off to buy some odds and ends. When she came out of the shop she realized her car had been stolen, and promptly rang her cell phone, which she had left in the car. The thief answered the call, whereby she explained that she needed the car to get her son to the doctor's office. Between the two of them, it was arranged that the thief would leave the car at a designated place, quickly disappear, and she would carry on her day as planned!

- Joy riding is becoming more common in the UK—youths steal your car, take it for a (usually rough) drive around town, and then abandon it miles away. Protect yourself by always locking your car, shutting all windows even when it's hot, and activating any car alarm you may have. The practice of "cracking" the windows of cars in the summer to keep them from overheating just isn't done in the UK.

- As a tourist, you should keep your money wallet close to your body at all times. Pickpockets are numerous at tourist attractions, and usually work in teams of at least two. Typically one thief will "bump" into you, and while he or she is apologizing, the second will have taken your wallet. They are unbelievably slick. The only thing you can do to avoid this is to zip up all bags and purses, and carry them in front rather than swinging from your shoulder or behind you, back-pack style. Also, do not wear expensive jewelry on display when walking through crowded streets, as this can be ripped from you in a heartbeat.

- Corruption is relatively rare in the UK, especially in politics. Judges, mayors, and so on are appointed, not elected, so the argument is that there is less need for bribery. Although high-profile politicians have had their fair share of scandals in the past, these tend to center on extramarital affairs rather than large-scale political extortion or bribery. Sometimes these scandals result in a resignation and newspaper head-lines.

- There is no national police force in the UK—they are divided into regional forces, although most wear the same uniform. The beat police in the UK do not carry guns; they carry truncheons, which are like billy clubs. Only specially trained police carry authorized firearms, and only as a last resort.

- Expect a completely different, and sometimes hostile, attitude toward the whole question of guns and gun control. It is very difficult to get your hands on weapons in the UK, and people are not used to the thought of either owning a gun or being hurt by one. Similarly, since capital punishment does not exist in the UK, you might find yourself in a few heated debates over this issue, whether or not you agree with it.

- 999 is the British equivalent of 911.

The vocabulary surrounding the world of crime is very colorful, but also quite different from the slang used in the States. Since American "cop" shows are so popular in the UK, the Brits may understand your slang, but I'm almost certain many of their words will leave you scratching your head.

BRITISH WORDS THAT MIGHT REQUIRE TRANSLATION

At Her Majesty's Pleasure—an indefinite stay in prison
A.W.O.L.—absent without leave
Bent *a*—crooked

The Bill—a reference to a TV drama show about the police

Bizzies *n*—the police (especially in Liverpool)

Black Maria *n*—large, black police van

Bobby *n*—policeman

Burgle *v*—to burglarize

CID—Criminal Investigation Department

Constable *n*—officer; old-fashioned salutation—"Good evening, Constable."

Copper *n*—police officer

Fiddle *v*—to cheat/embezzle (e.g., fiddling your expenses) (**On the fiddle**—to be involved in some form of embezzlement)

Filch *v*—to steal

Filth *n*—the police

Fuzz *n*—the police

GBH (Grievous bodily harm)—technically a criminal offense, but also used in common parlance

Grass *v*—to inform

Grass *n*—an informant

In the nick—in prison

Jam sandwich *n*—police car (so called because the cars are white with a red line along the middle)

The Met *n*—Metropolitan Police (London)

MI5—National Security Service, equivalent of the FBI

MI6—Secret Intelligence Service, international affairs, equivalent of the CIA

Nick *v*—to steal

Nick *n*—prison

Nicked ("You're nicked") *a*—caught, arrested

NSPCC—National Society for the Prevention of Cruelty to Children

Old Bill *n*—the police

Panda car *n*—police car (black and white)

Pigs *n*—the police

Pinch *v*—to steal

Plod—police officer (named after the PC Plod character in kids' Noddy books by Enid Blyton)

Porridge *n*—stretch of time in prison

Ram-raid *n*—ramming a stolen car into a storefront

Rat on (someone) *v*—to turn someone in

Rip-off *n/v*—swindle

RSPCA—Royal Society for the Prevention of Cruelty to Animals

Sleeping policeman *n*—speed bump

Tea Leaf *v*—thief (Cockney rhyming slang)

Truncheon *n*—billy club

Z Cars (pronounced "Zed" cars)—reference to an old TV drama series about the police

999—911

AMERICAN WORDS THAT THE BRITS DON'T SHARE

Burglarize *v*—to burgle

On the lam—not used

Paddy wagon—Black Maria

RESOURCES

www.MI5.gov.uk—MI5's official Web site

21

Naughty Bits

ANOTHER THING YOU'LL NOTICE fairly quickly in the UK is the penchant (pronounced "ponshon") for boobs, bums, and double entendres. Although *The Benny Hill Show* hasn't graced the TV screens for a good while there, his spirit lives on, as you'll discover. There will always be a debate about how liberal or conservative the Brits are, especially with regard to sex, nudity, and other naughtiness, but here are a few examples of things you won't quite believe you're witnessing.

TELEVISION

As I mentioned in chapter 10, "That's Entertainment," after 9 p.m. there is quite often full frontal nudity, explicit sex, and "adult" humor on TV. However, even before this watershed, I often find myself diving for the "off" button to prevent serious emotional damage to my offspring. The soaps in particular (which seem to be on every channel, all evening) have storylines full of illegitimacy, extramarital affairs, and drunken brawls. Admittedly in 2004, the media were beginning to ask whether the soaps were a little too unsavory, given their early evening time slots. I'm not sure the British public shared this concern, though.

Sitcoms in particular are adept at introducing bottoms, boobs, farts, and other such schoolboy humor at every opportunity. There's a lot of innuendo even in family entertainment, so be careful what you let your kids watch. Serious drama very often also means serious sex and explicit language, so be warned. Even the commercials may leave you utterly "gob-smacked" as there are many sexual overtones even for such seemingly innocent products as fabric softener and chocolate. The stand-up comics take a no-holds-barred approach to their material, which is frequently broadcast on national TV, albeit usually late in the evening. I recently watched a well-known British entertainer called Jim Davidson, and still cannot believe what he gets away with.

NEWSPAPERS

You've probably already heard that the British press is world-famous for its often truly awful headlines and questionable standards of reporting. What you may not be prepared for, however, are the "Page Three Girls," found in the more salubrious tabloids. Turn the front cover of these rags and there she'll be in all her topless glory, leaving very little to the imagination. Because they appear in national newspapers, several of these Page Three Girls have gone on to carve out successful careers as "TV personalities."

HUMOR/HUMOUR

Since my husband regularly refers to "that British sense of humor," I'll allow that it is different from the American, and often quite baffling to foreigners. Apart from the heavy-handed sarcasm that often confuses Americans, the Brits love their double entendres and will never pass up the chance to take the conversation down the avenue of sexual innuendo. "As the actress said to the bishop" is often added whenever something slightly suggestive is mentioned. Another oft-repeated phrase is Monty Python's "Nudge nudge, wink, wink." Whatever the phrase of choice, the Brits will flog a risqué joke to death, never tiring of its juvenile quality. In the summer between high school and university, I worked in a factory where the humor was often X-rated. My fellow (non-student) workers all found it hilarious that I was headed for Bristol University and would fall about the place whenever the subject arose (which they ensured was almost every day). You see, Bristol City is the Cockney rhyming slang for "titty"; this, in turn, is simply shortened to "Bristols"—hence the mirth.

There's a special kind of humor which you rarely find anywhere other than the UK, and that is the "camp" variety. "Camp" can mean anything from mildly effeminate to outright transvestite entertainment. For decades, male comedians have made their living either through extremely effeminate behavior or by being female impersonators. We're not simply talking about drag queens here, though; these men are usually excellent comedy entertainers, whether on the screen or stage. Catch phrases that you will still hear in general conversation hark back to the golden age of Saturday night variety TV shows featuring many of these individuals. In fact, here's a little quiz that you can have your British friends try:

Match the "camp" catch phrase to the comedian—

"Shut that door!"	Julian Clary
"I'm free!"	Frankie Howard
"Ooh err!"	Larry Grayson
"I thank you"	John Inman

Today's crop of male entertainers trading on their sexual ambiguity include Eddie Izzard, a very masculine stand-up comic and actor, who just happens to like wearing women's clothing and full makeup. Izzard, however, sounds like a bloke and stands like a bloke. Listen to him on his Web site at www.eddieizzard.com and you'll see what I mean. Julian Clary, another comedian and TV personality with a penchant for full makeup and sparkly clothes, is extremely camp and suggestive in his delivery. You can hear him on www.julianclary.net. Paul O'Grady made his name through his alter ego, Lily Savage. Lily was a loud, brash, and funny Liverpudlian (see chapter 1 on "Regions and Their Differences"), who was often invited onto game shows in her own right. Sadly, she has recently been retired by O'Grady. Graham Norton delivers yet another form of camp humor through his late night talk show, which can be seen in the States on BBC America. Although he follows the classic format of opening monologue plus guests and sometimes silly pranks and games, the humor is at all times just this side of scandalous and his delivery outrageous. The difference between today's camp comedians and those of yesteryear is that public non-acceptance of homosexuality then meant that many comedians had to live a difficult double life and went to great lengths to hide their "secret." You can read about "camp" humor and many of its best-known ambassadors at www.campaschristmas.com.

The Brits have long been amused by the sight of men dressed up as women, and the more camp the better. Whenever there's any kind of costume party ("fancy dress party"), you are guaranteed to find at least one burly bloke wearing his wife's frilly nightdress or old school uniform, plastered in makeup, and sporting false boobs. Thinking back to Monty Python, the usual image that comes to mind is of one or all of the team members speaking in ridiculous falsetto voices, pretending to be women. Since I'm not a psychologist, I have no idea why British men feel the need to don lipstick and stockings from time to time—but I know you'll witness the phenomenon yourself if you stick around long enough.

SCANDALS

The UK has its fair share of sex scandals. However despite heroic efforts by the media to raise a public outcry, the Brits usually find the whole thing mildly amusing or faintly disgusting, depending on the individuals involved. Many a male politician has had a photo of his "love child" plastered all over the press. The revelation is usually followed by a discreet disappearance from the glare of the camera, and all is forgotten. In 2004 the Home Secretary, David Blunkett, was discovered to have been engaged in a long affair with a married woman. What forced him to resign however, was not the scandalous relationship, but the fact that e-mails emerged suggesting that the visa application for his ex-lover's nanny had been fast-tracked. The lesson here is obviously never to jump the line in the UK!

A few years ago, Edwina Currie (author and former Conservative cabinet minister) revealed in a tell-all autobiography that she and John Major (Maggie Thatcher's successor as Prime Minister) had carried on a long-standing affair when they were both married to other people. The reaction of the British public was, at best, mild distaste at the mental images conjured up and a slight elevation (excuse the pun) of Mr. Major in the "stud" league tables. The big scandal in the summer of 2004—despite heightened security threats, Olympic Games, and surprising humidity in the South of England—was the affairs which Sven Eriksson had had in recent years. Sven, as the manager of the England football team, was better known than any politician could ever hope to be. His behavior caused a furor in the press and ructions in the management of the team, threatening the very future of English football. It was even commented on during the nightly national news for heaven's sake!

Prince Charles and his wife Camilla Parker-Bowles are largely left alone by the press these days. Before their marriage Camilla was openly cohabiting with Charles in his late grandmother's house, would you believe, and regularly appeared with him at official functions. On the other hand, we are still reading stories about the late Princess Diana's alleged love affairs after all this time, so the British public's interest probably depends on the glamour of the individual concerned.

DATING

Given my status as wife and mother of three children, this section was vicariously researched! I have many friends and relatives on the dating scene in the UK who keep me up to date. Among young people, dating becomes fairly monogamous as soon as you "go out with" someone. If someone asks you out and you accept, it is not the done thing to then go off and date other people, unless you are intending to be deceitful and gain yourself a reputation. Typically, if women date more than one guy, they are given a label such as "slag," even if they were up front about how many guys they were dating. (Incidentally, when a guy does the same, he is just "sowing his oats" and is expected to settle down when he meets the right person.) The idea of casual dating that is commonplace amongst American youth is not part of growing up in the UK.

Among older people, say over thirty, there seems to be more of a tendency to date someone with no commitment to see them again. Perhaps this is because anyone over thirty has no time to waste if he/she is searching for a partner. These people also seem to be much more willing to use online dating agencies and meet someone for a drink that way. I know several people who have done this, although most of them went in with the attitude that it was fun to meet new people rather than hoping to find their soulmate—which none of them has, as yet.

LOVE AND MARRIAGE

I do notice that "living together" is much more common in the UK among couples of all ages and, dare I say, classes. I know quite a few couples (with children) who have never tied the knot, and this no longer raises eyebrows. Gay and lesbian couples are an increasingly common occurrence, although there is the usual moral outcry from a few groups. In England and Wales, The Civil Partnership Act now gives same sex couples legal recognition of their relationship and confers legal protection in many of the areas now pertaining to married couples. Another event that hit the headlines in the summer of 2004 was the Scottish Bed and Breakfast owner who refused to allow a gay couple to sleep in the same bed at his establishment. He was happy to rent them a room with twin beds, but not a double bed! Despite the negative publicity he received in the press, and threats to disbar him from the Bed and Breakfast Association (or whatever it's called), he stuck to his ground. In general, however, hoteliers will rent a room to anyone who can pay the rate.

Love and marriage in the UK is a lot less "mushy" than in the States. You don't get as many people writing their own wedding vows and the speeches at the wedding are usually funny rather than serious and heartfelt. I have yet to hear a British priest or JP (justice of the peace) declare, "You may now kiss the bride," as part of the service. The most you'll get is the encouraging but rather embarrassed suggestion, "Go on, why don't you give her a kiss now?" Although a few blokes will sky-dive carrying a six-foot declaration of their love for someone (or otherwise get themselves on local TV for that purpose), most chaps are very averse to even letting people know that they are in love. If you're a demonstrative person and are known to canoodle in public, you might hear the mild reprimand, "No PDA here, you know!" PDA means Public Display of Affection, which is culturally forbidden in the UK.

NUDITY

As we saw in chapter 15, your average British female thinks nothing of going topless on the beach, whatever the years have done to her boobs. They usually do this "on the Continent" (e.g., France, Spain, and Greece), but since these beaches are full of

Brits anyway, they still run the risk of running into the mailman or their kid's teacher. There are several nudist beaches in the UK, which I'm told are very popular despite the inclement weather. Refreshingly, nudity in the UK is not just for the lithe, young, and tanned. People over forty, or even well into the twilight years, have been known to bare all in the name of authentic drama. Witness the recent success of the movies *Calendar Girls* and *The Full Monty,* where many of the lead roles were filled by mature actors. In London, the stage production of *The Graduate* had established actresses of a certain age queuing up to take on the roll of Mrs. Robinson, despite the fact that it required full frontal nudity.

SEX

Where do I begin? As already mentioned, I'm not a sociologist, anthropologist, or any other brainy type, and am therefore as much in the dark about British sexuality as the next person. The stereotype of the stiff-upper-lip, "No Sex, Please, We're British" type still springs instantly to mind, but one look at the section that follows demonstrates that the British at least think about sex a lot! How else would they have that many words for it, and for the body parts involved? I hasten to add that this is not an exhaustive list, just the ones I could bring myself to put down on paper. After all, my mother or my children could read this book.

There are frequent, interminable "polls" in various British newspapers asking such thought-provoking questions as how British men rate themselves in the sex/romance stakes (why not just ask the women?) or how British men compare with their Mediterranean counterparts. Personally, it all strikes me as a little paranoid—a case of too much talk and not enough action—but that would be introducing a degree of subjectivity that I have so far managed to avoid. However, now that I'm being subjective, I might add that I find the attitude to sex, nudity, etc., far more relaxed in the UK than in the USA—although I do live in the Midwest. As with everywhere else, though, there are "moral majority" groups who aim to keep the country on the straight and narrow and lament loudly when they fear the worst.

Astonishingly, in December 2003, Scotland's Roman Catholic Cardinal Keith O'Brien was moved to announce that the UK was in danger of going to Hell in a hand basket: "Are we just going to progressively decline into a Bacchanalian state where everyone is just concerned with their own pleasures and to sleep with whomever they want? The future at times does look quite bleak on this." This is not quite the Britain most foreigners imagine, is it? And then, as if to illustrate his point, on a 2004 *Big Brother* show (which seemed to be compulsive viewing for everyone), a couple were heard to be having intercourse under the dining table, hidden by a tablecloth or blanket. Although there did seem to be a collective intake of breath over this, the media blew it up to such a degree that it was difficult to gauge whether the public were really very outraged at all. In true British fashion, the show was not threatened with being taken off the air as might have happened in the States.

BRITISH WORDS THAT MIGHT
REQUIRE TRANSLATION

Arse *n*—ass
Arse-licker *n*—brown-noser

Arse over elbow—falling over oneself, or back to front

Arse over tit—same as above

*__Bee stings__ *n*—small boobs

Bent *a*—crooked; homosexual

"Bent as a nine bob note"—homosexual

*__Big girls' blouse__ *n*—someone acting effeminately or just rather hopeless at something

Bird *n*—female

*__"Blow me!"__—expression of surprise

Bollocks *n*—testicles, but also used like "Bullshit"

Bonk *n & v*—sexual intercourse

*__Brothel creepers__ *n*—shoes with thick crepe souls

Bristols (or Bristol Cities) *n*—Cockney rhyming slang for titties

*__Bum__ *n*—bottom

*__Cock-up__ *n & v*—a mess

*__Crown jewels__ *n*—male privates

*__Crumpet__ *n*—foxy-looking woman

Dog's bollocks—something that's really good ("It's the dog's bollocks")

Dickhead *n*—literally, penishead

*__Fag__ *n*—cigarette

Fairy *n*—homosexual

Fanny *n*—female genitalia

Goolies *n*—testicles

*__Hanky-panky__ *n*—mutual, and enjoyable, sex

Hump *v*—to have sex with

*__John Thomas__—the penis

Knackers *n*—testicles

---

* These words can usually be used without causing offense, but the rest should be used with extreme caution.

Knickers *n*—ladies' panties

Knob *n*—willy

Knockers *n*—boobs

Knock up *v*—sometimes means to wake someone up in the morning, can also mean to get someone pregnant

Legover *n*—to have sex with someone (getting your leg over)

Loaded *a*—very well off (doesn't mean drunk)

Ponce *n*—homosexual

Poofter/Poof *n*—homosexual

Randy *a*—horny

Roger *v*—to have sex with

Rubber *n*—eraser

Rumpy pumpy *n*—mutual, enjoyable sex

Shag *n & v*—sexual intercourse

Shirtlifter *n*—homosexual

Slag *n*—loose woman

Slag (someone) off *v*—to gossip or insult someone

Slapper *n*—loose woman

Slap and tickle *n*—fooling around

Slash *n*—pee

Snog *n & v*—to make out

Stiffy *n*—erection

Stonker *n*—erection

Tadger/todger *n*—penis

Talent *n*—attractive members of the opposite sex

Tool *n*—penis

Totty *n*—attractive women

Tosser *n*—jerk

Tosspot *n*—jerk

Twat *n*—female genitalia, but usually used to insult someone

Up the duff *a*—pregnant

Up the spout *a*—pregnant
Wank *n & v*—masturbation
Wanker *n*—jerk
Wazz *n*—pee
***Willy** *n*—penis

AMERICAN WORDS THAT THE BRITS DON'T SHARE (SOME OF WHICH SOUND UNINTENTIONALLY RUDE)

Bone up on something
Buns (meaning butt)
Hickey
Ho (meaning whore)
Shagging flies
Weiner (either for food or the you know what)

Modesty precludes including the most obscene words and phrases. My advice in this potential minefield is to abstain from using British words until you are sure of their appropriateness. As you can see, even the most innocent-sounding American words can have huge shock value in the UK. I would also strongly advise reading the first few chapters if you haven't already done so.

22

Miscellany . . . and Manners

THERE ARE a few points that don't seem to fit into any specific place, thus we have the dreaded "miscellaneous" chapter. However, I believe these points are important for Americans wishing to make the most of their stay in the UK.

MANNERS

I find it amusing that many Americans think the Brits are extremely polite, and that many Brits, on visiting the States, return the compliment about Americans. Part of that is because (unless you live in London) most people like tourists. In the case of Brits, tourists who speak almost the same language are even better. I'm still on the fence about which race is the more polite, and anyway, it doesn't really matter. There are a few areas, though, where as an American, you will definitely come across as rude, even though your intentions could be saintly.

I have mentioned many specific examples in the opening chapters of this book—innocent words and phrases that can cause confusion, embarrassment, or laughter. Consider yourself duly warned that the single rudest thing you can do is to refer to a person (while they are present) as "he" or "she." Similarly, if you are ordering for everyone while in a restaurant, don't say, "*She* will have the omelets," or, "*They* would like the cheese-cake." I know it seems silly, and I know that Americans mean no offense by it, but most Brits won't know this and it will come across as incredibly rude.

Please

Still on manners—you will soon notice that the Brits say "please" all the time, even when they are hurling insults at each other or voicing extreme displeasure. As kids, insulting one's siblings always seemed less worthy of punishment if we had coupled the insult with a loud "please," as in "*Please* shut your mouth and don't come near me ever again!" On the other hand, if you have time before your trip to the UK, take note of how rarely Americans actually *say* the word "please." Again, I know that the thought is conveyed in your intonation, and if you're from the South, the preamble to any request surely indicates graciousness. (I'm talking about phrases such as "Could you go ahead and pass me the doohickey.") Unfortunately, Brits throughout the land expect to hear "please" and, in the case of children, may even go so far as to correct the omission on a few occasions.

Thank You

Conversely, Americans make a much bigger deal of saying "Thank you" than the Brits. As is common in almost every country, everyone is expected to say "Thank you" in the UK, but it ends there. At the most, a Brit might say, "That's okay," or, "No problem," when thanked, but you'll rarely hear, "Mmm hmmm," or, "You're very welcome." In fact, if you answer a thanks with the usual American "Mmm hmmm," you might even hear a few titters. Don't be offended either by this or by the fact that people rarely acknowledge your thank you's; that's just the way it is, and no offense is intended.

Sorry

Another word you'll hear a lot in the UK is "sorry," and it has a million and one uses. My American husband and his colleagues find it hilarious that you can barrel through a packed train station or airport terminal, knocking everyone down in your wake but as long as you are yelling "sorry" it's acceptable. Indeed you might find people parting to let you through. If the "sorry" isn't heard though, you'll hear mutterings of "Cheek!" and perhaps people may even deliberately impede you to teach you better manners.

Brits apologize even when it's not their fault. To illustrate this, Kate Fox a British social anthropologist, did a hilarious experiment in her book *Watching the English: The Hidden Rules of English Behaviour* (Hodder & Stoughton, Ltd., 2004). In crowded places like stores and train stations, she pretended to be distracted and then deliberately bumped into people, with quite some force. A large percentage of her "bumpees" apologized even though the collision was clearly her fault. A few years ago I made a complete fool of myself by reacting in this very British way. Going through an airport security line, a female employee pointed out (somewhat officiously I have to say) that I had a wad of notes sticking out of the jacket I had just removed. I immediately apologized before she laughingly reminded me, and everyone else within earshot, that I had done nothing wrong.

"Sorry" is also used when someone hasn't heard you, when he or she wants to squeeze past you, or when someone is trying to attract your attention. What you won't hear the word used for is to express sympathy. In the States, we often hear "I'm so sorry that it rained on your wedding day" or to a child "I'm sorry that the pool is closed today." When I first heard this use I racked my brains for quite a while trying to figure out the connection between the person apologizing and the actual event. The Brits instead will say, "It's such a shame it rained on your wedding day," or "What a pity the pool is closed today."

Timeliness Is Next to Godliness

You'd think this was the correct adage judging by the Brits' fixation for being on time. I'm not saying everyone actually manages never to be late; indeed, many of my friends have yet to achieve that, but on the whole, punctuality is a much bigger thing in the UK. If the Brits are late, they rarely make their entrance without apologizing profusely and giving you intimate details of the event that caused them to be delayed. While this may seem ridiculous to you, meet them halfway and at least apologize if you're late. After all, you have kept them waiting,

and the Brits read into this that something else was more important than them. Basically, late is rude.

Excuses, Excuses

Talking about profuse apologies and detailed excuses, the Brits
will rarely decline an invitation without telling you exactly why
they can't make it to your shindig. Even if they're telling a fib, it
will be meticulously researched and fairly unlikely to get them
busted. Having spent a lot of time with Americans, most of
whom will simply say, "Sorry we can't make it, but thank you
for inviting us," I now find it amusing to watch the lengths the
Brits will go to in their efforts to make sure they don't give offense. As an American in this situation, while you don't have to
divulge the details of your social calendar when declining an invitation, be prepared for a long silence when you RSVP in the
negative, as your would-be host will be expecting some grovel-
ing on your part.

THE END JUSTIFIES THE MEANS

Brits, on the whole, are less forceful about their individual needs,
especially when in a group setting. (I am not saying that this is a
good thing, necessarily.) For example, if you're sightseeing with
a group of Brits, you might find yourself the only one *not* saying,
"I don't mind, I'll do what everyone else wants to do," or, "I'm
easy," when faced with the decision of what to do or see next.
Given the resulting lack of action at this point, you'll probably
get a tad impatient and feel the need to voice a preference just to

get things moving. If the atmosphere becomes slightly frosty, it's probably because you had the gall to "put your needs first"—but no one will say this to your face. I would ignore it if I were you. As long as you aren't rude or insulting in voicing a preference, you probably saved hours of debate or procrastination, I can't decide which! What does come across as rather unsporting is if you were to abandon the group and do your own thing, when the original plan had been to sightsee as a group. The Brits choose a "give and take" approach in these situations.

As I mentioned in chapter 9, when visiting someone's home, don't voice too many requests, as many Americans ask for stuff that the Brits just don't have, such as ice, iced tea, and *real* coffee. This results in general embarrassment all round. The trick when asked what you'd like is to ask what the host *has*. By doing this, you'll come across as a much more pleasant guest and avoid disappointment at the same time. As a houseguest, make sure to keep your hosts informed of your activities; going on a day's sightseeing without telling them when you're leaving and what time you're coming back is considered very rude. (You should probably invite them along, even though they'll most likely refuse.) If you get up in the morning before your hosts, and can't wait around for them to appear, leave a note apologizing and give an estimated time of return. (This makes things easier for anyone expecting to cook you a meal, as well as just being good manners.) Hopefully, this will sound like common sense to you, but I know of more than one American staying with Brits who has unwittingly treated the house like a hotel. Although the Brits love to put themselves out for others, they don't like to be walked all over. If you offend them, you'll probably never be confronted about it but the air could become decidedly frosty.

VOICING DISCONTENT

The Brits are notoriously bad at voicing discontent. Whether it's appalling service in a restaurant, being let down by a "friend," or suffering a personally humiliating experience at work, they can rarely summon up the nerve to confront the person at fault. Instead, they have perfected the art of "seething" and "sending someone to Coventry," whereby the person who has caused the offense will simply be completely ignored, probably forever more.

As a potential offender (and you'll now realize the *huge* potential here), just be on the lookout for averted eyes and deafening silences—a sure sign you've transgressed some unspoken rule. Even when you ask what the problem is, you'll likely hear, "Oh nothing (sniff)," as the injured reply. At this point you can take one of two approaches: either happily say, "Oh good," and put the matter to rest; or shame your silent accuser into confession with something like "Look, it's obvious you're upset with me, but I have no idea why unless you tell me." Unfortunately, without knowing the person involved, I can't predict success in either case. Good luck!

PSYCHO-BABBLE

The Brits are not nearly as "in touch" with their feelings as Americans like to think they are. In general conversation, you usually won't hear words like "psyche," "modus operandi," and "self-actualization," and conversations can get very uncomfortable if you insist on sharing your therapy experiences with Brits. Showing the true British "stiff upper lip," most Brits don't go into therapy to help deal with life's crises (although some probably should); conversely, their favorite American stereotype is that all Americans go into therapy at the first whiff of disappointment.

OFF TO BEDFORDSHIRE

If you read the opening chapter, on "Regions and Their Differences," you'll know that Bedfordshire is pronounced "Bedfd-sha," but the Brits also use this word as another word for plain old "bed." My point about beds is that, on the whole, Brits rise and go to bed later than many people in the States. Even my friends with young kids seem never to go to bed before about 11 p.m. When socializing in the evening, you'll often find that people meet up later by at least an hour, and no one really does much before 10 a.m. at the weekends. Just something to bear in mind when making arrangements.

PACE OF LIFE

In general, I would say that the pace of life in the UK is slower then that in the United States, with perhaps the exception of London. Many Brits visiting the States comment on how everyone is perpetually on the go, with or without small children. In the UK, weekends, in particular, are fairly laid-back affairs. The slower pace will cause you some frustration at times, but hey—you could be in Italy, Spain, or Greece, where things *really* slow down!

CULTURE SHOCK

After more than fifteen years in the States, I still haven't decided whether the UK is surprisingly similar or very different. The countries probably have two of the most similar cultures in the world but if all you see are the differences, here's some advice; enjoy, even embrace them. Lamenting the things you miss or going on about how it's better in the States won't change a thing, will irritate everyone around you, and, most importantly, will prevent you from enjoying your British experience. It's a country full of history, charm, quirkiness, and beauty, so just remember your umbrella and "Enjoy!" One final note—if you think the Brits sound hilarious when attempting an American accent, just remember that your rendition of the British accent is probably the same in reverse!

RESOURCES

www.britainusa.com—Official Web page of the British government in the USA

www.travelbritain.org—Web site for Americans traveling to Britain

www.knowhere.co.uk—Contains information on over 2,000 places in the UK, from pubs to skateboard parks

www.information-britain.co.uk—An extensive site for tourists, with information on travel, plus subjects like restaurants and shopping